D1473643

IT CAME
FROM THE
SWAMP

IT CAME
FROM THE
SWAMP

YOUR FEDERAL
GOVERNMENT
AT WORK

·

SUSAN
TRAUSCH

BOSTON   1986

HOUGHTON MIFFLIN COMPANY

Library of Congress Cataloging-in-Publication Data

Trausch, Susan.
It came from the swamp.
1. United States — Politics and government — Anecdotes, facetiae, satire, etc. 2. Washington (D.C.) — Social life and customs — Anecdotes, facetiae, satire, etc.
I. Title.
JK289.T7 1986   320.973   85-30511
ISBN 0-395-38466-4

FOR DAD

ACKNOWLEDGMENTS

STOP! Don't skip this page. Think how you'd feel if you had your name in the acknowledgments and people flipped past it because they thought it was the dull part.

This stuff is important and I'm keeping it short. No lists of grade school teachers or rhapsodies to my first singing coach. I never took singing lessons.

Just the hard-core "without whom" group, and there is always such a group with any book because nobody writes one of these babies alone.

It only feels that way.

And so many, many thanks and warm thoughts to:

Arthur Hepner, who called one otherwise blah Monday morning in September 1984 and said, "So, why don't you do a book on Washington?" (If you've got any complaints, talk to Arthur.)

My editors, Robie Macauley and Larry Cooper, and the folks at Houghton Mifflin, for their help, ideas, and encouragement.

The *Boston Globe*, for being a good friend over the years and for turning me loose for six months.

Joanna Pratt, Steve Samuels, and Evan, for all the dinners and movies and for making me feel at home on an alien planet.

Eileen McNamara, for the laughter and for being able to see all the naked emperors.

John Stobierski, for being New Hampshire amid the penguin suits.

My mother, for a lifetime of support and love.

CONTENTS

IT CAME
FROM THE
SWAMP

1

It Came
from the Swamp

IN 1790 OUR FOREFATHERS looked out across a vast new nation and decided to build the capital of the United States in a swamp.

Hard to believe, isn't it? There they were, surrounded by forests and mountains and lakes and several hundred square miles of prime oceanfront property, and they set up shop in a bog on the Potomac.

"How could this be?" you may be asking yourself. "These were bright guys who ran a terrific little revolution and wrote some great stuff and they're sounding like my brother-in-law."

The answer is simple: they took a vote.

Any time you get a bunch of politicians together for a vote they're going to sound like your brother-in-law. They'll deliberate for hours, days, or years, and then come up with a plan that will most likely put the whole deal smack in the middle of a stinking fen. This is called "compromise," mainly because the people involved are usually compromising themselves when they pass the legislation.

Washington, D.C., was forged in compromise and consequently never had a chance. It was doomed from the day it was conceived in the minds of people who should have known better and who obviously did know better, because most of them built their homes out of town on high ground. You think Thomas Jefferson ever once considered putting Monticello on K Street? Get serious.

As any fool knows, with the exception of your brother-in-law and the rest of the people who bought time-share condominiums in Lake Okeechobee, swampland is a bad investment. Things tend to sink in swamps. Things like the Washington Monument, for instance, which the National Oceanic and Atmospheric Administration reports may be going down. They're not sure yet. They're doing tests. This is typical. In Washington nobody ever has a clear sense of what is actually disappearing into the muck or merely settling into a more advantageous position. We'll know for certain in another three hundred years or so. Maybe.

The National Oceanic and Atmospheric Administration has to be one of the silliest departmental titles in the U.S. government, and that's going some. It shows how the thinking works around here. Ocean and air are administrable, you see. The tides, the stars, the planets, and the entire universe can be departmentalized and managed from an agency in Washington, D.C.

Which brings us to the other major problem with building in swamps — they're haunted and do strange things to the mind. Think of the horror flicks you have seen in your lifetime. At least half of them involved swamps, right? There's a reason for that. The inexplicable lurks in the murky, muddy places of the earth. Weird shapes bubble up in the night, or in the afternoon for that matter, and then unleash themselves on the citizenry. Either that or the citizenry ventures into the swamp and is eaten whole by a pack of reptiles with a glandular disorder.

Mists and gasses breed here that befuddle the brain and cloud the vision. Now you see it, now you don't. Half-submerged tree roots look like giant alligators, and giant alligators look like half-submerged tree roots. Walls of hanging moss beckon and then disappear. Beware the killer toad, the quick-

2

sand pit, and the crazed hermit plotting to take over the world from some remote rotting little shack.

Really, folks, this is not the sort of place you want to put your Internal Revenue Service.

On the other hand, maybe it is, but then don't be surprised when the 1040's are hard to read.

You build a capital in the swamp and you're plain inviting the bad vibes in for lunch. It's like walking the country under a ladder, or letting a half-dozen black cats loose to run across the flag at midnight, or jumping up and down on all the cracks on the way to Concord and Lexington.

It also drops a load of psychological fallout on the heads of those who try to live there. A capital that is summarily dumped into a swamp is never going to feel good about itself. No matter how big it grows or how pompous it sounds, there will always be that core of doubt, that feeling of inadequacy — constantly overcompensated for, but never quite eliminated — that one simply wasn't good enough for New York. A capital in a swamp will naturally take on the characteristics of its surroundings, turning in on itself like some bizarre ingrown toenail. It will get bogged down in maddening minutiae. It will see visions, very often of grandeur, and it will make about as much sense as the Everglades on a dark night.

As intelligent, thinking individuals our founding fathers knew all this, but when they voted in a group they had other fish to fry. That's how politics works. What appears to be blatantly stupid when viewed by a single person becomes politically viable when viewed by the Congress. It also becomes complex beyond recognition. You don't just say, "Okay, we need a capital, so let's put it over there and get on with the business of becoming the United States of America." You've got to plan it to death, talk it to death, and then mull it over and amend it.

Momentum for putting a capital somewhere in the United States began to grow around 1783. Seven years later Congress was ready to vote on it.

The whole thing had come about because the country was

having problems with its "floating seat," as it was known in the trade, and wanted one that was nailed down. There was no permanent headquarters for the government, and Congress was wandering from town to town like a nomadic tribe, unable to put down roots, build gymnasiums, or hire several thousand legislative assistants. They either took it with them in a sack or left it at home. They'd ride into New York or Trenton or Baltimore with their sacks, find a big hall with enough folding chairs, and then call the meeting to order.

This system worked fine until they got to Philadelphia one day in 1783 and ran up against a group of Revolutionary War veterans who were ticked off about not getting paid. The soldiers surrounded the hall and refused to let anybody out until they got their money. The siege went on for two days and two nights and is probably the first recorded instance of lobbying in this country. Congress kept yelling to the Pennsylvania militia for help but was told, in effect, "That's not my station — call the feds." When they finally got themselves loose, their first order of business was to vote to spring for their own hall and their own chairs in their own town. The idea was to create an enclave far from the madding crowd, where the government could do its work unhampered by reality.

The big question, of course, was "Where?" Every town in America raised its hand and said, "Over here, over here! We'll give you a deal on chairs." Much as Congress wanted a permanent home and a deal on chairs, it found itself in a pretty tough spot and spent the next six years trying to get out of it. In 1789 lawmakers reached a decision that would become popular with many a future legislator in a similarly tight spot: they decided to punt.

By a vote of 23 to 17 they issued the following decree: "That a permanent residence ought to be fixed for the general government of the United States at some convenient place as near the center of wealth, population and extent of territory as may be consistent with the convenience to the navigation of the Atlantic Ocean."

4

Oh yes, and that it should be no farther north than New York and no farther south than Virginia.

The legislation offended no one, solved nothing, and sounded like Harvard Law School. Congress patted itself on the back and adjourned, leaving the matter for the next session.

In June of 1790, perhaps weary from another winter of wandering around schlepping sacks, lawmakers hunkered down over their lexicons and passed an amendment. The result was a revision in the 1789 decision, which read as follows: "That a permanent residence ought to be fixed for the general government of the United States on the River Potomac at some place between the mouth of the Eastern Branch and Connogochegue."

Wherever that was and however it was pronounced, the amendment obviously got things cooking, because a month later Congress managed to go the whole nine yards and pass what became known as "the Act Establishing the Temporary and Permanent Seat of the Government of the United States."

Ta-da!

Just one problem, and those of you who are still awake may have spotted it. A temporary and permanent seat is a contradiction in terms. A government is either sitting for keeps or it's not, and it can't do both on the same chair.

But with Congress anything is possible. What they did was create two seats: one in Philadelphia, which had a lot of popular support despite the unpleasantness of 1783, or maybe because of it; and the other to be carved out of swampland donated by Virginia and Maryland. Philadelphia would be the capital for ten years, to give the city enough of a grip on history to develop some legitimate tourist attractions and print up the "They Wrote It Here!" Independence Hall T-shirts. The Southerners would get the permanent capital, to make them feel better about having to help foot the bills for the Revolutionary War, after the folks in Massachusetts started it.

5

So by 1790 everybody was as happy as could be expected under the circumstances, except for the Powhatan Indians. They lived in the swamp. They'd been knocked around by the white man quite a bit already, but this was too much. The Bureau of Indian Affairs right in their back yard. There goes the neighborhood.

They sought revenge, preferably for eternity, and set in motion events that put the absolute kiss of death on the District of Columbia — as if it didn't have enough problems already. Late one dank fall night in 1790 a group of the tribe's elders met with the wise and powerful medicine man. The medicine man knew the dark secrets of the swamp as well as he knew the foibles of human nature, and the combination was unbeatable. Sitting on a log with the fetid air swirling in clouds around his feet, he held his left hand high and said solemnly, "We are going to fix those suckers." He then went into a trance, calling forth the forces of the bog. The muck bubbled up, the trees swayed, and the ground shook. A deep and fearsome moan echoed through the land, and a voice spoke out of the gloom:

"Beware all who enter this place, for it shall ever after be a monument to absurdity. It shall operate according to its own laws and folkways, making fools of those who think they can rule here. Their number shall be many and their folly great, for they shall be intense and without humor and never notice what is happening to them. They shall run forever in circles carrying water in pails without bottoms to paper forests of unquenchable fires. They shall speak in windy voices that only fan the fires and say nothing. And they shall believe that they are the center of the universe when the rest of the country is really more interested in watching *Love Boat*. This means you, Alexander Haig."

The voice dissolved into a thunderclap, and then there was silence. The band of Indians packed up their things, herded their families together, and left before the bureaucrats descended upon them.

In 1800, as the government journeyed from the temporary bosom of Philadelphia to settle in its new home between the mouth of the Eastern Branch and Connogochegue, people were struck with the blinding flash of insight that comes with first impressions: they never should have left Philadelphia. Washington, D.C., was the pits. The town had mosquitoes you could put a leash on, cockroaches that could walk the mosquitoes, and mud up to here. It was hot and filthy and generally considered a great place to go on a Saturday night if you needed a case of malaria. It was so bad that foreign ambassadors who came here got combat pay.

"For this we sat through seven years of congressional debate?" people asked each other as they stood around the streets looking for a four-star restaurant. But it soon became obvious that they would have to build one. They would have to build a lot of things, and from the ground up.

"Let's get a French guy to design a really knockout plan that will make us forget we live in a hell hole," somebody suggested. "You know those French — lots of sweeping boulevards and parks and hauteur that'll blow your socks off."

"*What* that'll blow your socks off?" a couple of people asked.

"Hauteur."

Enter the architect Pierre Charles L'Enfant, whom a few confused individuals addressed as "Mr. Hauteur" while they kept a close eye on their socks. L'Enfant didn't care, though, because he was creating a masterpiece. He ran around town with his sketch book, stood on the tops of carriages waving his arms, and regularly shouted "Mon Dieu! Magnifique!" to himself as he got bright idea after bright idea.

Now, if you've done a fair amount of shopping in your life you know that bright ideas from France don't come cheap. The U.S. Congress didn't know this, however, or at least said it didn't know, and figured it could work some kind of deal. After all, L'Enfant was doing a whole city. He could afford to work at cost, no?

No. L'Enfant didn't give discounts. He unveiled his pièce de résistance, handed the government a $95,000 tab, and then stood there with his arms folded, drumming his fingers on his coat sleeves like an imperious waiter.

George Washington took him aside and said, "Listen, Chuck, we're a new country. We've got a war to pay for. We just can't come up with this kind of cabbage right now. We were thinking more along the lines of twenty-five hundred bucks — three thousand max. How about we make the streets smaller and bag the marble staircases?"

L'Enfant flung his plans across the room and left in a terrible huff. This was a mistake he would always regret. Congress picked up the blueprints and took them to an independent contractor who implemented most of L'Enfant's ideas for a fraction of the cost. The Frenchman, who by this time was shouting a lot more than "Mon Dieu!" and "Magnifique!" took the government to court but never got a cent for his work. He did, however, have a fairly nice plaza named after him in the southwest section of the city. It is also a stop on the subway. The Yellow Line.

Relations have never been quite right between America and France, and I have a feeling the friction may have started here. It didn't do much for our image in Europe, either. Getting L'Enfant's plans for zip may have played well in some circles, but generally speaking, the diplomatic community was not amused. We were the boobs on the international block, uncultured clods with muddy boots and no manners who didn't know from marble staircases.

We didn't know much from national security, either, as it turned out. In our first big war as an independent country we almost gave away the store. Fighting the British in 1814, our military leaders decided it was okay for the troops to leave the capital unprotected because the British would never attack D.C. "Come on — the capital?!" said the generals. "They'd have to be crazy to march in here. If they attack anywhere, it's going to be New York." The British marched straight into

D.C. and nearly flattened the place. A guy named Murphy, the inventor of the law that bears his name, came along with them, and his descendents have made their home in Washington ever since.

Over the next hundred-and-seventy-some years the District of Columbia shoveled muck, stomped bugs, bought screens, installed air conditioning, built the Kennedy Center, spawned the bureaucracy, and developed that unmistakable aura of superiority evident in places where people who once wore muddy boots now know how to pronounce "hauteur."

It was a strange metamorphosis, though, and in many ways evolved into a sort of municipal version of *The Picture of Dorian Gray*. For as the city became more and more pleasing to the eye — buildings gleamed and statues decorated the traffic circles and flower beds sprang up in the parks — the minds of the people who lived here became more and more twisted and sick. They began to think of themselves as the focal point of the planet, and then eventually as existing on a separate planet all their own from which they directed the comings and goings of the galaxy.

Unlike the Dorian Gray legend, in which the lead character knows he's in trouble and keeps his secret locked away in an attic, the Washington story unfolded with very little self-recrimination. To this day, the city has no conception of itself as being weird. It displays its soul every night on the evening news and thinks the picture is a study in dignity. It watches but doesn't see, and it listens but doesn't hear.

Snatches of conversation float mystifyingly in the air like captions in a *New Yorker* cartoon, but no one notices.

"You can't pay any attention to the national weather reports if you live in Washington," a woman at a party says authoritatively, shoulders back, head high. "We're too far south and too far north for those things to affect us."

The people around her nod in agreement. This makes perfect sense to them. They are in another dimension, and all is as it should be. Of course. No problem. The national weather reports affect the entire U.S. of A., but not Washington. Not with the National Oceanic and Atmospheric Administration running the show.

Washington is an unreal place, a district carved out of bad land, a living irony that hosts the entire federal government but has no voting members in Congress representing itself. It is a diamond-shaped Twilight Zone floating in limbo between North and South, circling forever in its own orbit, cursed, crazed, and haunted.

Literally haunted. Every historic city has ghost stories, but there is an edge to them here that I never felt in Boston. Walk down the wide, dark halls of the Old Executive Office Building and you can feel the shadows and are convinced you're hearing too many footsteps echoing behind you.

In October 1984 I spent a rainy afternoon in the Capitol tracking Daniel Webster's ghost for a feature on haunted places in Washington. The Capitol has always scared the hell out of me anyway, with its twisting hallways and labyrinthine stairways and endless rows of unmarked doors, so I wasn't surprised when workmen remodeling a remote area on the third floor swore they'd seen the long-dead Massachusetts senator sitting at an old desk. The area, which Webster had used for storage, was in the guts of the original Senate wing, up a maze of stairways. It had been redone for Senator Patrick Leahy of Vermont, and I asked one of his aides to show me around. We stood in a quiet nook where the chandelier cast odd shapes on the high ceiling, and our voices sounded as though we were speaking into microphones. No phantoms materialized, but one seemed to be seriously considering the prospect. Standing within the walls of the past, listening to the muffled sounds of the modern-day government somewhere far away, I felt like a ghost myself, hovering between two worlds.

Working in the Capitol late at night, I would often shiver in a deserted hallway, whip around quickly to see no one there, and walk briskly through Statuary Hall, where General Robert E. Lee is said to appear regularly to shake hands with General Ulysses S. Grant. They say John Quincy Adams haunts the old House chamber, where he suffered his fatal stroke while delivering a speech; and a stonemason, murdered on the job, supposedly walks the basement rooms, scraping the walls with his trowel.

Okay, laugh if you want to, but all I can tell you is that at eleven o'clock at night it ain't funny. Remember, this is the town where novelist William Peter Blatty got the idea for writing *The Exorcist*.

Blatty was a student at Georgetown University in 1949 when he read articles about a priest performing an exorcism on a fourteen-year-old boy who lived in Mount Ranier, a Maryland neighborhood just across the northeast D.C. line. The boy was said to cause furniture to move, objects to fly across the room, and scratching noises to sound in the walls of his home. Although that house was destroyed in a fire and the property is now a vacant lot, the area is still known as "a neighborhood of tragedy," according to an article in the May 6, 1985, *Washington Post*, which outlined a series of violent crimes that continue to plague the residents. Double murders, mummified bodies in closets, a man suddenly dropping into a coma and dying, unexplained fires and suicides — it's all there if Blatty is looking for material for a sequel.

And if he needs any more inspiration, he should check out the D.C. Metro's lost and found. I mean, we are talking strange down there. Subway riders in other cities may drop the traditional umbrella or briefcase or hat, but here, well . . . Officials at Washington's lost and found report finding false teeth, diamond rings, television sets, a saddle, a bridle, boots, shoes, crutches, wheelchairs, a crate of live chickens, and a coffee-table edition of the Kama Sutra. They have also found a toilet in a box.

I say it's poltergeists hitting the trains late at night. Believe me, this stuff does not come from the rush hour crowd. All those people do is read newspapers, write reports, and try to keep their trench coats from wrinkling. No, this debris is sent from somewhere else, out there, deep in the swamp, probably from the dark and plotting heart of Rock Creek Park.

To me the park is Swamp Central. It is here that the ancient Indian spirits hang out and laugh. Take one of the steep dips down into the beautiful but tortuously convoluted forested roads that run through the District's lush underbelly, and there can be little doubt that that place is spooked. I have driven through Rock Creek for several years now and still get lost, still go white-knuckled around the hairpin turns, still miss the unmarked exits spinning off blind curves. And I have yet to find Maryland, although they tell me it's down there.

Directions for getting into Rock Creek are never clear. It just sort of creeps up on you. Drive down an innocent-looking residential street, and suddenly there you are, surrounded by the park. I always have the feeling that it is trying to take over the city, quietly encroaching on the northwest streets, sending up long, aggressive vines, and snakes and killer raccoons.

Washington has had a problem with rabid raccoons for several years now, and I think one almost got me outside my apartment building. It was either rabid or possessed. I was coming home from work one night, walking through the pool area of the apartment complex, when I saw the animal sitting on a knee-high stone wall. I stopped about six feet away and stared at him as he stared at me and didn't move. This seemed to be a good indication that he was a nut case because animals usually run. I slowly backed up a couple of feet and he walked forward. Definitely a nut case. Clutching my briefcase tightly, hunching forward in the work dress, and thanking the powers that be that I was wearing those ridiculous jogging shoes, I turned around and ran for my life, looking like a crazed yuppie. Then I glanced over my shoulder and saw that the raccoon was tearing along the wall after me.

I felt terrified and idiotic at the same time. This was surreal. In the center of civilization, the very pulse of the military-industrial complex, surrounded by high-rise buildings containing every modern convenience known to man, a human being was being bullied by a small furry creature that couldn't even operate a personal computer.

I hit the street and ducked into a supermarket, out of breath. A few people stared questioningly, but I wasn't about to shout, "Rabid raccoon! Head for the meat freezer!" Besides, he was gone, vanished, you might say, into the night, no doubt scurrying back down a ravine to join his diabolical little pals in the park.

Yes, the curse of the swamp lives and grows. It is with us every day in matters public and private, infusing the very air with its ancient magic.

I went to a lecture on occult phenomena at Washington's Open University, where the instructor quite casually explained that Washington is probably one of the most haunted cities in the country. He said the placement of the District on the border between North and South has made it a magnet for things that go bump in the night.

"Go out into the woods where Civil War battles took place and fire a gun into the air," he suggested. "You'll hear running footsteps and rustling in the leaves. The fact is, there are a lot of spirits floating around Washington who simply don't know the war is over."

I believe it. And I think some of them have been elected.

2

They Did
What?

"HOW DO YOU LIKE living in Washington?" people who don't live here keep asking, and I'm not sure where to start.

The first thought that comes to mind is a one-liner from some comedian whose name I can't remember, but the joke goes: "Other than that, Mrs. Lincoln, how did you like the play?"

Can a person "like" living in Washington? Is it living? Did Alice enjoy falling down a hole? Is it good for a person to space-walk without a suit?

No, but you can get used to it. Sort of. Although hanging suspended upside down somewhere east of reality can work up a terrific pain in the neck, and in other parts of the anatomy too numerous to mention. The trick to living in Washington is to realize you've hit a plane of existence that is absolutely incapable of functioning like a normal city. It is in the grip of forces beyond its control, not the least of which is a deep and brooding geographical neurosis.

I'm talking about this North-South business. "A city of northern charm and southern efficiency," somebody once said, but it wasn't John F. Kennedy, the experts tell me, although he is usually credited with it. The phrase continually comes up in conversation here, indicating a certain world view and self-image that can only mean these people do not know where they are at. Located south of the Mason-Dixon line and north of Appomattox, the District of Columbia straddles two regions, four quadrants, and several hundred mindsets about what that means.

Is Washington a northern city or a southern city, and how much either way? Is it supposed to lean back and pass the black-eyed peas or whip up a smart little brie and broccoli quiche? Should it relax and say "y'all" or march around like General Sherman? The decades have passed and the questions have gone unanswered, leaving the citizens to drift and create Washington as we know it today — a city with the fastest bureaucratic foul-ups in the East and the slowest snow plows.

Make that "plow." The District of Columbia has one snow plow and it's broken. They don't believe in snow here. After all, this is the South, right? Washington has a clause written into its charter saying that snow falls in places like Buffalo and Boston and Minneapolis in the winter and that it can't happen here. So whenever it happens and a flake actually hits the pavement, the whole town turns into Chicken Little. People huddle together at their office windows, look fearfully down at the street, and wonder if they will get home alive. If they are at home when the flake hits, they stay there and make sure they have extra canned goods in the cupboard. Schools are closed, the government starts announcing its "liberal arrival–liberal leave policies" — which only the government understands — and the city dispatches its broken snow plow to the White House to protect the President. People can be slipping and sliding on the side streets, but the plow will be moving meticulously back and forth in front of 1600 Pennsylvania Avenue, even though the guy who lives there has a private plane on his roof.

I remember my first snowstorm in D.C. — and there is usually one hummer every year despite the clause in the charter. I looked out the apartment window and assumed the street

15

would be plowed sometime that day. A month later, when it still hadn't been plowed, I got the idea — the city was waiting for it to melt. Washington is famous for its summers, not its winters, and there is an August mentality that says the heat and humidity can take care of everything.

Each year the pattern remains the same. The blizzards come, the blizzards go. The cars without snow tires pile into each other during the rush hour. The people go bootless to work on a January day when the sky looks like slate. And it doesn't occur to anyone to say, "Gee, we seem to be getting snow here, maybe we should prepare ourselves for the inevitable." Oh, no. That would make sense. That would disrupt the system.

Everything in Washington operates according to an intricate, carefully worked out system. That's why nothing makes sense.

I'm thinking right now of the letter the IRS wrote to my uncle after he died. They had a question about a tax form he'd filed two years before and wanted another copy of it. My mother was handling his affairs and sent the government a letter explaining that he was dead, and enclosed a copy of the tax form as well as a death certificate.

A few weeks later the IRS wrote back, addressing the letter to my uncle. They returned his death certificate and income tax papers along with something called "Government Form 3699 — Return of Documents to Taxpayer." On it the appropriate box had been checked to indicate that the tax papers and the death certificate were indeed being returned and that he should "please keep them for your records."

The letter read as follows:

Dear Mr. Willesch:

Thank you for your reply to our inquiry about your form 1040 of 1982. The information reported to us is shown on the attached sheet.

Please use the enclosed forms 1040 to file your return

within 30 days. You may use the enclosed envelope to mail the forms to us.

If you write us again, please give us a telephone number where you may be reached during normal working hours in case we need more information.

The system, in all its intricate, carefully worked out glory. Brisk, numerical, documented in triplicate, it sits down and writes letters to a dead man.

Welcome to Lewis Carroll country. Living here means taking a deep breath every few hours, stepping back, closing your eyes, and saying, "Okay, who ate the funny mushroom? Was it me or was it them?" It is usually them, unless you have lived here too long. Of course, if you have lived here too long, you wouldn't be asking the questions because then everything would make sense, even the $400 hammer.

By now all of America has heard of the $400 hammers and the $700 coffee pots and the $500 toilet seats and other outrageous overcharges billed to the Pentagon by defense contractors. The government had been paying these rates for years and would probably still be paying them if somebody hadn't decided to go to the hardware store one day and price hammers. That may sound like a fairly obvious course of action to you and one you would have taken the minute the hammer salesman showed up in the sharkskin suit. But Washington has never done well with the obvious. The obvious is too simple, and Washington thinks in the complex.

Although the public usually learns about this kind of thinking only after it erupts into major news, months of hearings, and demands for legislative reform, it is actually a way of life that is routinely accepted, hardly noticed, and rarely reformed. It is rooted deep in the minutiae of every day, beginning with morning coffee and staying on through the late show.

The most mundane activities can develop dense bureaucratic overlays that make them almost unrecognizable. Crossing the street at K and Nineteenth, for instance, requires a

17

lawyer and a ruling from the Department of Transportation. The city has posted directions telling people how to cross and what the "Walk/Don't Walk" signals mean. Not a totally outlandish idea, I suppose, except when you consider that the directions are written in very small print and tacked to utility poles on traffic islands in the middle of the street. Which means a pedestrian doesn't get any help crossing the street until he's halfway across.

The signs read as follows:

1. WALK — Okay to cross
2. Flashing WALK — Start crossing and watch for cars
3. Flashing DON'T WALK — Don't start, but finish crossing if you've started
4. Steady DON'T WALK — Pedestrians should not be in crosswalk

Okay, so say a person crosses from the curb to the traffic island on a flashing DON'T WALK and then reads the directions telling him he should not have started across the street. Does the conscientious citizen go back to the curb or hang around the island waiting for a WALK? And what happens if someone starts across on a flashing WALK, gets as far as the island, and then has the light change to a flashing DON'T WALK? The sign says to "finish crossing if you've started," but is the start considered to be the corner curb or the island? And, finally, if someone is concentrating on getting across K Street without tripping over the island or being killed by the drivers making left and right turns, is that person really going to have the time or inclination to read the signs in small print tacked to utility poles in the middle of the street?

I know that a committee must have worked for months, possibly years, designing the street-crossing directions on K Street. The Environmental Protection Agency and the White House were probably involved. Reports were written, consultants were called in, parameters were defined, and then when the dust cleared, the nation's capital had built another monument to craziness.

It happens all the time. Look at the Rayburn Building. That was carefully planned. Why do you think people have so much trouble finding the hearing rooms? The planners decided that every room on every floor would begin with the number 2, which makes about as much sense as having every room on every floor of the Longworth Building begin with the number 1.

When a constituent comes to town to shake hands with his representative in room 2441 Rayburn, his instincts will take him directly to the second floor, where he will then spend the rest of the afternoon wandering around, because room 2441 is on the fourth floor. In the Rayburn Building the *second* number in the room number sequence indicates the floor. Ditto for the Longworth Building, but not for any of the other buildings on the Hill.

Don't look too hard for the logic here because you'll hurt yourself. Just remember that if any of your friends or relatives disappear in Washington, check the Rayburn Building first. They're either on the second floor or they're running up and down a back stairway, following the exit signs that lead to doors that don't open. A tour group from Pittsburgh went in the Rayburn Building last spring and still hasn't come out.

Life in nongovernment buildings can get just as weird as it does in federal ones. A friend of mine lived in an apartment building where the janitor spent most of his time planning and developing his managerial strategy. He called himself the "building systems supervisor" and acted as though he were running a small country. He sent memos to the tenants outlining what he called "the total systems concept" of residential management and even had his stationery imprinted with the letters TSC. He explained that under his plan, all maintenance needs would be evaluated and prioritized according to the needs of the system as a whole. It wasn't just a matter of fixing the broken window; it was a matter of assessing whether the window was more or less important than the furnace, and then whether the broken mailbox lock took precedence over the heat.

"What it meant," said my friend, "was that you waited eight months to have your dishwasher fixed."

I worked in a downtown office building that was run by a team of environmental engineers, several supervisors, and a computer. The result was an office with no air. They just didn't do air in there. They were too busy evaluating the environmental quality.

The building had two temperatures — too hot and too cold. Whenever anybody complained, the team of engineers and supervisors came in with electronic heat-sensing equipment, waved a magic wand around the room, and said, "It's seventy degrees in here — should be no problem." It didn't matter whether you were too hot or too cold. They always ended the discussion by saying "It's seventy degrees in here — should be no problem."

One day the building fire alarm went off and I called the management office fully expecting to hear that it was seventy degrees and no problem. Instead, the person answering the phone said simply, "I can't help you. We don't get involved with the alarm system." I suggested that if the building was burning down, we'd all be getting involved with the alarm system, and could she please tell me if this was for real or a false alarm. She told me to call the security service, which was located in Virginia. At that point I decided to get the hell out of there and ask questions later.

The woman in the management office was one of the rule keepers. The city is full of them — stiff-backed, precise people clinging fiercely to the established procedure because it is the only thing between them and chaos. They know they are living in the Twilight Zone, and at any minute the center could fly off into outer space. So they don't look left and they don't look right. They just cite the rule, usually several times, repeating it as though it were a mantra, even if the building is on fire.

I think that may explain the reasoning behind the FBI telephone bomb threat questionnaire. Then again, it may not.

The telephone bomb threat questionnaire was developed by the FBI Bomb Data Center, which collects information on bombs and prints it once a year in something called the *Bomb Summary*. The questionnaire is on a long green card that the center hands out to government and private-sector workers so that they can keep it near their phones and be ready with a procedure whenever a mad bomber calls.

I've never personally talked to a mad bomber, but have a feeling the conversation would not go as smoothly as the questionnaire seems to suggest it might. I think that maybe when a person started asking the cuckoo on the phone the nine suggested bomb threat questions fresh from the FBI Bomb Data Center, he would either laugh his head off or plant another bomb.

The questions run like this:

1. When is the bomb going to explode?
2. Where is it right now?
3. What does it look like?
4. What kind of bomb is it?
5. What will cause it to explode?
6. Did you place the bomb?
7. Why?
8. What is your address?
9. What is your name?

And if there's time before the thing goes off, be sure to get a social security number and two references.

Security types seem to have no sense of timing or of human nature. Take the Federal Emergency Management Agency. That's the group that spends its days planning where everybody should go in case of a nuclear attack. They've decided to put half of Washington on the Beltway and send us to Maryland. Should be an interesting drill: considering how well this city handles itself in snow, fallout will be a piece of cake.

I try not to think about national security. It makes me feel insecure. All those experts staying up late studying contingency plans for every disaster and alternatives for every eventuality, keeping the citadel of democracy locked, guarded, and fail-safed — they're too much like a Peter Sellers movie. And no matter how late they stay up, there is always the inevitable, red-faced, toe-curling "oops!" in the morning. The State Department looks around and announces that — oops! — by golly, it has just let a load of secret documents accidentally slip out the door to the prisoners at Lorton Reformatory.

Lorton Reformatory is a D.C. correctional institution in Virginia. The State Department is a U.S. diplomatic institution in Washington. Normally, the two don't have much to do with each other, but in 1983 the State Department decided to send the prison a bunch of surplus file cabinets, which was a very nice gesture, except that the government forgot to take the classified documents out of the cabinets before sending them up the river.

The matter was investigated for months, and the FBI was called in. The agency found that surplus memory typewriters had also gone to the prison and that the memories had not been cleared of secret briefing papers. In addition, the Department of Energy had sent over a couch for refurbishing that had some classified documents on nuclear weapons stuffed back behind the cushions.

As a spokesman for the State Department told the *Washington Post*, the problem was the fault of no one in particular, but of "the system as a whole." In other words, oops! People were so busy having the proper forms approved and following the strict procedure for moving government furniture out of secure areas that they simply forgot to look in the drawers for secret stuff.

It's like the slip-up that occurred during the 1985 inauguration ceremonies. Amid the tightest security in the history of the U.S. presidency, some guy from Denver wanders into the White House with the Marine orchestra. Just wanders in while the Secret Service and armed forces have the place surrounded, every manhole cover in the city bolted shut, and antiaircraft missiles on red alert.

"It was a breach of security," a Secret Service spokesman told the *Washington Post*. "We're doing an internal evaluation."

Oops!

Meanwhile, over at the Washington Navy Yard they don't mess around. They shoot the Christmas vodka on sight and ask questions later.

When Soviet naval attaché Lieutenant Commander Vladimir Antsiferov dropped by the yard with some friendly holiday cheer for his American counterpart in December 1984, the guards at the gate didn't recognize him and didn't take any chances. They were trained. They had a system. This was a Russian with a package, so they shifted swiftly into Armageddon mode. They ran the bundle by some bomb-sniffing dogs who barked, put it through an x-ray machine that revealed "two liquid-filled canisters," and then called the 67th Explosive Ordnance Disposal Team of the Military District of Washington to blow that juice right out of the sky.

. . . And Happy New Year to Mrs. Antsiferov and the kids.

This is the way the world will end, folks. One day somebody is going to get a fruit cake in the mail and hit the button.

Ah, Washington, home of the freaked, land of the barricade, where there's a system for everything, and it works perfectly until you need it. Overprogrammed, perverse, bizarre, the city is a continual assault on the laws of logic. Where else can you stand on the corner, hail a taxi to go to Capitol Hill, and wind up in Virginia?

I'm serious. This happens. The District is loaded with cabbies who can't speak English, most of them driving illegally, who have no idea how to get there from here. City authorities seem to have no interest in clamping down on the situation, either. Maybe because they've been too busy fixing the snow plow.

I got in a cab at National Airport one night to go to D.C.,

was taken into the District, and abruptly whipped back out to Virginia on Route 66. All the while the cabbie kept shouting, "I know the way, I know the way!" That sentence and the word "yes" turned out to be the only English he knew. With a series of hand signals, I got him turned around in Rosslyn and back into Washington, but it was a long night.

Not as long as the night I spent on the phone with the D.C. police department, however. That one stands out as the ultimate northern charm–southern efficiency story, and if I ever have to call them again, I'm going to head straight for the deep end of the Potomac.

It began four days before Christmas at 11:30 at night when I discovered that someone was parked illegally in my underground garage space at the apartment building. I had just gotten home from dinner at a friend's house and was supposed to catch an early plane the next morning to go home for the holidays. This is a lousy time to discover someone else's car in the assigned and paid-for spot you've been using for two years, although there is probably no particularly good time for such a discovery.

Not wishing to park in another person's assigned and paid-for spot and, as they say in Washington, "exacerbate the situation," I called the authorities. A brisk, efficient D.C. police officer answered the phone and the conversation went very well.

"No problem," he said. "We'll have someone right over."

I had such confidence in him that I went and sat in the lobby, figuring any minute the cops would come and do justice. I sat there until 12:30 and then began to have doubts. I called the police department back, but this time the conversation did not go well.

"Hello," I said to a second brisk, efficient officer. "I called an hour ago about an illegally parked car."

"Yes, ma'am," he said. "That's been checked out."

"Checked out?" I asked.

"Yes, ma'am," he said.

"You mean you've been here?" I asked.

"I didn't say that, ma'am," he corrected. "I said it's been checked out."

"How do you mean 'it's been checked out'?" I asked.

"It's been cleared," he said, still brisk, still efficient.

"But the car is still in my parking space."

"We handle these calls by priority," he said. "They come up on a computer screen and they're taken in order."

"And my call has been taken care of?"

"It's been cleared, ma'am," he said.

I took a deep breath and tried again. "Are you saying that somebody in a uniform physically came into my garage and actually looked at the car parked illegally in my parking space and then placed a ticket on said offending vehicle?"

"No, ma'am," he explained. "I said we cleared the call. That means we put it on the computer screen and we'll get to it when we can. Illegally parked cars are a low priority. It'll probably be quite a while."

I hung up and tried to process what I'd just heard while simultaneously concentrating very hard on not ripping the phone out of the wall. With the murky reasoning that human beings back themselves into in the wee hours of the morning when they should be alseep, I decided that calling the police department back again would be a good idea because I might get that nice officer who had said, "No problem, we'll be right over," and then everything would be all right.

I rang the department and got a third officer, who had a "look kid, let me tell you how these things work" attitude. He told me to forget about going through the police department, and that I could save a lot of time by contacting a towing company directly. He even gave me the number of a towing service in my area.

"No way," the towing service guy shouted into the receiver after I explained the problem. "Nobody tows a car in this city until it's been ticketed. Have you called the police department?"

Like a moth to the flame, I hung up and did just that yet a fourth time. The officer who answered was more succinct than the others had been. He said that the police were really busy on Friday nights with murders, break-ins, and muggings, and that no one would be out to ticket the car. Ever. Period.

"But my call has been cleared," I said weakly.

"What?" he said.

I hung up and decided that the only thing left to do was exacerbate the situation. Somewhere around 1:30 A.M., I parked my car illegally and left a note on it explaining why it was there. I then gave a note and my car keys to the night clerk in the lobby so that he could give them to the management office the next day so that they could eventually move my car back into its proper space when the offending car was out of there.

Four hours later I got up, caught the plane home, called the management office after I arrived to explain things one more time, and then had a Merry Christmas. A week later I returned to Washington to find the bad car gone and my car back in its place. All seemed right with the world until I looked on the windshield.

There, briskly and efficiently tucked under a wiper blade, was a $25 parking ticket.

3

Workaholics
Unanimous

WASHINGTON IS OBVIOUSLY working too hard. Way too hard. So hard, in fact, that I think many parts of the city have lost contact with the planet Earth.

To say that people here are intense about their jobs does not begin to describe what goes on along the Washington career path. Obsessed is more like it. Warped is another word that comes to mind, as do bonkers and sick. We're talking about a breed that was born on a desk with a beeper in its navel and an umbilical cord attached to the telephone. Wired, they are. Plugged in. Strung out. Up and at it days, nights, weekends, and holidays, pushing to make the meeting, to make the contact, to make partner at the law firm, and to make a mess of what could be a very nice city if everybody in it went on vacation.

It mystifies me how Washington ever got a reputation for being a city of glamour, scintillation, and sex scandals. These people don't have time for glamour, scintillation, and sex scandals. They're too busy writing memos. Their idea of excitement is an all-night session on a tax bill. Their idea of a great meal is one that includes a business meeting, three committee reports, and a panel discussion. They wear navy blue suits, button-down oxford shirts, and maroon ties, and that goes for the guys, too.

Paris it ain't. More like Pittsburgh with monuments.

Sure, I know, Rita Jenrette did it on the Capitol steps, and Fanne Fox jumped into the Tidal Basin, and John Riggins shouted "Loosen up, Sandy baby" to Supreme Court Justice Sandra Day O'Connor at the 1985 Washington Press Club dinner. But why do you think that stuff is such big news around here? Because people are dying to read something besides the *Congressional Record,* that's why. Do you think any of those items would make the front page in L.A.? Page two or three, maybe. Probably the back of the book in a news roundup column. But here they give people hope. An occasional sex scandal sizzling across the front page of the *Washington Post* convinces people that they are not boring and that all kinds of wild and crazy parties are going on around them and that they'd be attending these orgies with bells on if they didn't have such responsible positions so high up in the government, with the eyes of the United States of America upon them.

It's not that people lead dull lives, exactly. They know a lot of fascinating facts about Tunisian import quotas, highway infrastructure, and natural gas consumption. But there's a certain lack of the old joie de vivre, if you know what I mean. When you hear about a lawyer who goes to a Halloween party in a Dracula costume and then spends the evening discussing a class-action suit with a clown and a couple of ghouls, you know you're dealing with a group that has trouble letting go.

No matter what the occasion or the dress, Washington workaholics gather in tight, tense little clusters to talk about how much pressure they're under at the office. It's as though they feel guilty about being in a place where somebody might see them having a good time. They figure God will get them if they make whoopee. Worse yet, they might miss *Agronsky and Company.*

I once overheard two people in a coffee shop discussing a

Tarzan movie they had seen as though it were a policy statement. They were leaning forward, elbows on the table, staring at each other with the intense look of White House aides who get to their jobs at 7 A.M.

"It's obvious," said one, making careful notes on a napkin. "Tarzan is the ultimate U.S. isolationist."

Where is Johnny Weissmuller when we need him?

These two were exhibiting what's known as "the Type A personality." Type A's are the people who killed themselves mustering out of "Group B" so they could come to Washington. And they didn't come here to relax in front of a big screen and eat popcorn. They came to turn themselves into zombies, destroy their marriages, and make America a better place.

Local newspapers and magazines regularly run stories on why Washington works so hard, why it can't have meaningful relationships, and why it usually winds up on a couch talking to somebody for seventy-five bucks an hour. The tone of these pieces is, "They live in Washington — you can't expect them to be normal."

In a February 1985 *Washingtonian* magazine story titled "Why Can't I Fall in Love?" authors Gail Friedman and Randy Rieland noted that "Washington is full of men and women on three- or four-year stints who don't want love to complicate their temporary stays." Among the many career people interviewed was a "top aide to a senator," whom they described as "consumed by his work, committed solely to the fortunes of his boss."

"Most of the powerful bosses in this town could care less about the quality of your relationships," the aide was quoted as saying. "All they care about is the quality of your relationship with them. . . . We think in terms of how many people we know, not how many people we know well."

In an October 1984 *Washington Weekly* story titled "Secret Sex — Washington's Sorry Love Life," Linda Levine, a therapist, observed that the city "is a place where people come to achieve, and a successful sex life simply isn't on the approved list of achievements."

A woman who was interviewed in the *New York Times* on April 11, 1985, lamented the lack of spontaneity in Washington. She said she had been asked out on a date by a government official who told her to call his administrative assistant to set up a time. The first available slot was in three weeks.

Talking with psychiatrists and psychologists for one of these stories of my own, I was told by the spokesman for the American Psychological Association that overachievement is "built into the culture here." He also said that he couldn't talk long because he was finishing a project and had just worked thirty days straight with no weekends off.

"There are some very sick people here," a psychiatrist told me, "but they function quite well in government jobs."

"People who come to Washington think winning is everything," said James Collins, chairman of the psychiatric department at Howard University Hospital. "Politicians are our gladiators, and this is their arena."

Maybe that explains what's going on at the YMCA pool.

They don't swim at the YMCA pool — they go for the gold, and it's about as relaxing as a tank of piranhas. There are two fast lanes, with the other lanes cruising at approximately the speed of light. Try to drift along and enjoy a leisurely side stroke, and someone'll swim right over you and tell you to go back to the plastic water wings.

Things were getting so hot and heavy there at one point that the pool management had to put up the following warning sign, or "advisory," as they no doubt called it:

> Swimming is not a contact sport. We urge you to use caution while swimming laps. This is not a war. If someone taps you on the feet it is not an insult but merely a swimmer's way of saying "Please let me pass."

Yeah, sure. More like, "Please let me pass or I'll break your goggles."

If the fun bunch isn't out trying to drown itself during recess, it's probably taking a grueling run around the Mall. Groups of co-workers tend to jog together so they can discuss the upcoming briefing in between side aches. Then they go somewhere for a working lunch. Actually, they "do lunch." That's the phrase, as in "Let's do lunch." Meals are strenuous activities. They are "done" like sit-ups or aerobics. They work. That's why they are called working lunches, working breakfasts, working dinners, and working snacks.

Washington has put the word "working" in front of every enjoyable noun in the English language. There is the working weekend, the working vacation, and the working coffee break. The Senate Foreign Relations Committee once posted a notice for a "closed working coffee on El Salvador," which sounds like something that would require the Heimlich maneuver.

The working meal was invented shortly before the discovery of the stomach ulcer and is just about as much fun. What happens is that anywhere from two to several hundred people come together and try to look intelligent while they're figuring out what to do with their olive pits. Put them on the edge of the salad plate and they invariably roll off. Put them in the ashtray and they look like someone's pet rabbit has been on the table. Drop them on the floor and people start to talk. You can't win with olive pits, or lasagna or Reuben sandwiches, which is why the really savvy working-meal people eat at their desks before leaving the office and then just order Perrier and limes.

The idea is to look fast, trim, and aggressive at these gatherings and not drip anything on your notes. I have not mastered this — fast, trim, aggressive, or dry notes — and have always felt that if God had wanted the stomach and brain to work at the same time, he would have combined them into one organ. There would have been an opening in the tops of our heads for pouring food directly into the gray matter so it could turn quickly into brilliant thought. But the way things are set up, food goes down and away from the brain to an entirely different section of the body and turns into gas. People who try to mix these two functions are asking for trouble. Perhaps this is why the expression "full of hot air" originated in Washington.

Just reading the discussion topics scheduled for working meals is enough to give a person indigestion. Notices are posted for "the Toxic Waste Breakfast," or "the War on Drugs Buffet," or "the Transportation Table Luncheon," and people are expected to sign up in droves, and do.

The worst one for me was a "Reye's Syndrome Lunch," at which representatives of the aspirin industry talked to a half-dozen reporters for two hours, trying to convince them that the product was not linked to the disease despite tests indicating the contrary. I was suckered into going because the group came from Boston and sounded like news. It wasn't. It was indigestion. We were given reports, testimonials, charts, and everything but color slides, along with a seven-course Chinese meal that went down like a bottle of dry aspirin.

On another occasion I sat staring at a slab of beef while a State Department official talked about war in Lebanon. The guy had been invited as the inside source of another reporter at work, and the dinner was considered a coup. It was indeed impressive, but I wish we could have had something a little lighter to go with death and destruction, like Tuna Surprise, maybe, or watercress salad. Even better would have been meeting in the afternoon over a cup of black coffee. Of course, these high-powered types aren't available in the afternoon because they're working way too hard to take a break and, supposedly, so is the press. That's what makes the working meal so exciting, especially if it's a dinner. Participants sit down knowing they're indispensable because they couldn't possibly have scheduled this important meeting any earlier than nine o'clock at night.

The ultimate in late-night working meals is the annual White House Correspondents' Dinner, which is not only after dark, but on a Saturday and in black tie. Held each spring and sponsored by the White House Correspondents' Association, the dinner brings together just about every reporter in Washington with just about every source so they can pump each other for information. The President and the First Lady are seated at the head table with assorted White House Correspondents' Association honchos, guest speakers, and heavy hangers-on. Every news organization in the city buys a table in the cavernous Washington Hilton ballroom and then tries to outdo one another with impressive guest lists. Lavish cocktail parties are thrown before and after the dinner, again for the purpose of courting and flaunting impressive guests. In 1985 the *Los Angeles Times* won the court-and-flaunt award hands down when it threw a tented extravaganza out in a courtyard of the hotel and rang people to chow with a huge Chinese gong.

Although this may sound like a hot night in the old town, these people are not having a good time. Believe me, I've been there. Nobody ever has a good time wearing a cummerbund. What you've got at these feeds is a couple of thousand penguin suits all vying for a position next to the key players in the power structure so that they can exchange business cards and try to set up another working meal as soon as possible.

The idea is to have a working meal every night of the week and, preferably, three times a day. I know a man who really does this. He has lived in a condo for three years and brags about how he has never used his kitchen. He hasn't bought any furniture, either. He's got a bed, a desk, and four blank, echoing walls that look out at the sky through curtainless windows. He gets home every night at eleven or twelve, travels a lot, and says he doesn't have time to shop.

"When do you relax?" I asked him.

"I don't," he said, frowning slightly at the word "relax" as though it had a slight odor.

I used to work with a reporter who would get insulted if you suggested he take time off. He prided himself on never leaving the Hill press gallery before the wee hours, and had a wife and two children who saw him only at breakfast. When vacation time came, he packed his family off for the shore and joined them a week or so later to give himself time to "clear a few things off my desk."

Clearing off his desk required a steam shovel. He let everything pile up from the last vacation and never opened his mail. So he'd sit there pale, thin, and grim, surrounded by two trash barrels and a leaf bag, sorting through the rubble and discovering assignments that would keep him away from the beach for another week.

People have this feeling that if they leave Washington, the republic will collapse — or, more to the point, that it won't. Three days before Christmas I sat in a boarding area at National Airport waiting for a plane to Florida with a group that was in a veritable swivet over the republic. They stood in a line waiting to use the pay phone so they could call their offices and make a last-minute check on various projects that would be checked on again when they landed.

"This will involve the State Department," a man said tensely into the receiver. He was wearing a Mickey Mouse sweatshirt and his daughter played with a Cabbage Patch doll at his feet, but his mind was not going to be contemplating dancing sugarplums anytime soon. He would be taking the State Department with him to Walt Disney World and would hit every phone booth in the park.

This crowd has a thing about being near the phone like you wouldn't believe. They queue up at public booths in discos, restaurants, theaters, health clubs, and other places where most normal human beings have no desire to talk to the office. They balance their briefcases on the narrow phone booth shelf, take out papers, and write stuff down as the curtain is going up on the second act or as the entrée arrives. And when they get back to their seats their beepers go off, so they have to leave again and get back to the phone.

The phone fetish runs so deep that some people can't go to the bathroom without one. On my first trip to D.C. I stayed in the Hay-Adams Hotel, where the bellhop pointed out the features of the room and indicated the telephone next to the toilet as though he were showing me the extra soap packets.

Maybe I hadn't lived, but it was the first one I'd seen, and I didn't want to talk to anybody on it. What exactly is phone protocol in such a situation anyway, and what does one say when it rings — "Hi, I was just thinking of you"?

Such indelicacies don't seem to bother a city that thinks of itself as one vast work space. Many hotels, some businesses, and private homes have telephones in the bathroom. The Capitol Hill telephone directory tacked in the press gallery's phone booths even lists a number for a bathroom in the Russell Senate Office Building. Unable to ignore such madness, I dialed it once to see what would happen.

It rang.

"Hello," a man's voice answered.

"Hello," I said.

"Did you wish to speak to someone?" he said.

"Yes," I said.

"Who?" he asked, the impatience creeping into his voice.

I scanned the names on the directory and blurted out, "Senator Proxmire," hoping he wasn't there.

"He's not here," the man said.

"Excuse me," I said, dropping the charade, "but I actually called this number to find out why you have a phone in the Russell bathroom and what sort of bathroom it is."

There was a cold, dead silence.

"We have a phone here so we can take calls. I'm really very busy and don't have time to answer questions," he snapped and hung up.

No doubt he was taking a working shower.

The professional code of the Hill in Washington says that successful people should always be doing two, and preferably three, things at once, and that they should try to be in several places at the same time. Members of Congress, for instance, have their staff assistants fill every minute of the day with schedules that only a hyperactive child or a megalomaniac could love.

A computerized study done on the Hill a few years ago showed that on one day more than a thousand meetings took place at the same hour, and there are more now. Consequently, legislators bounce around from committee room to committee room to constituents to closed working coffees and, of course, to the floor to vote on the vital issues of our time without being too sure what they're doing. A staff member usually briefs them quickly before they go into a room so they know if they're supposed to look grave or wave and shake hands.

Ronald Reagan may have tried to set a new pace with his nine-to-five presidency, but the people around him haven't bought the program. The earlier one rises and the longer one stays awake, the more status one is supposed to have. The *New York Times* regularly runs "working profiles" on these compulsives, and most of them come off sounding like the Incredible Bionic Bureaucrat.

Take the one the paper did on Assistant Attorney General Robert A. McConnell in October 1984. Leslie Maitland Werner reported that McConnell was in the streets and jogging by 4 A.M. and at his desk by 5:30. He usually worked until 7 P.M. and liked to put in "at least one day each weekend."

At least? The last time I counted there were only two days, total, in the weekend, but then I go by the twenty-four-hour clock. Washington clocks have forty-eight hours, and the Bureau of Standards is developing one with seventy-two.

Nothing lights the fires of these people quite like working through an entire day and an entire night. Back in school we used to call this "pulling an all-nighter." In Washington they call it "the all-night session," which is not as colorful, but what can you expect from older folks who stay up too late?

I went to an all-night session once. It was a House-Senate conference on the 1982 tax bill, and it was a cross between a Monopoly game, a marathon, and a pajama party. Members of the committee came together in a room that was too small and too hot to put a tax bill into final form while every lobbyist in America tried to get their attention. People sat in clusters, came in and out of doors signaling thumbs up or thumbs down, traded Park Place for Boardwalk until the sun came up, and seemed to be having the time of their lives.

"This is psychological warfare," one lobbyist said, smiling broadly. "It's one side trying to wear the other side down. It's the American way."

A woman who represented educators, and had been doing these gigs for eleven years, said she felt the all-night sessions forced people to hunker down and get the job done. "This way, they know they can't go home until they reach a decision. You don't agree at eight o'clock at night," she said, "but things sound a lot better at four o'clock in the morning."

They were there at four in the morning, and at five and six, and at seven, eight, and nine. They ate junk food all night and slept in folding chairs and felt proud of themselves for hanging tough.

I hung tough until around one in the morning and then left when my contact lenses fogged up.

Maybe these sessions are democracy at work, but to me they seem more like lunacy at full gallop. I wonder if our leaders have ever considered pacing themselves a little better so that they could be clear-headed instead of semiconscious when they make their decisions. Who knows? America could wind up with some intelligent tax legislation that way.

But working clear-headed is considered boring. The reason people take jobs in Washington is to feel a great weight of responsibility on their shoulders while fending off a crisis. If there's no crisis to fend off, they invent one by squeezing the time clock. Consulting-firm executives regularly tell clients they'll get eight-month projects done in six, and then expect the staff to make up the difference on weekends. Law firms expect everyone to give up a vacation at the whim of the senior partner, and White House aides figure they've just fallen off the mountain if they're told to take a break. So what we have here is a town of neurotic compulsives making national decisions on very little sleep.

If you want to get a sense of just how warped life is in the nation's capital, take a ride on the Metro during rush hour. The Metro is Washington in microcosm. Space age sleek and sterile, it is full of people in identical trench coats who are busy, busy, busy, reading reports, making notes on yellow pads, and holding staff meetings.

"The Grigsby case is going well," they say in deep, resonating tones as they sit together in clusters, open their briefcases, and pass papers around. I'm always surprised when they haven't Xeroxed enough copies for the whole subway car, since they obviously want to share their business with everybody on the train.

"I've got a tough schedule today," another person will say, "but let's try to touch bases around three-thirty."

"How did the briefing go?" someone else in the group asks.

"Not bad," comes the answer. "We're moving right along, but I don't think we should press this right now."

The urge is great to slap this guy on the back and shout, "Go for it and press, chicken liver. Remember, you swim at the YMCA!" But I control myself and keep taking notes. Nobody notices me because the trench coats assume everybody else is concentrating on his or her own projects that must be completed before the train reaches the station.

Passengers sit there working portable computers, adding long columns of numbers on calculators, and dictating into tape recorders. One morning a guy in the middle of a packed car was practicing his Italian along with a Berlitz tape. Oblivious of the crush around him, he just kept conjugating those verbs, or whatever one does with Italian verbs.

Meanwhile, a man seated in front of me was loudly reviewing his entire career as a consultant, telling his companions why he had quit.

"It was so wretchedly dishonest from top to bottom, I just had to get out," he said in a booming voice.

"The project simply was not economically feasible to continue but they pushed it," he said. "This was probably one of the largest, most important national projects I ever worked on. I don't want to give the details now because it was rather shocking."

Tune in tomorrow, straphangers, for another exciting episode of *All My Projects*. Join us again at 9 A.M. on the Red Line to find out how shocking the details were and just how large and important this project actually was.

Although passengers are generally tolerant of their fellows, the man playing a tape recording of a speech at full volume proved to be too much. He had the recorder on the seat next to him and would replay certain parts again and again as he took notes. Finally, a woman who was reading the *Washington Post* leaned over, obviously annoyed, and said, "Would you please turn that down? The rest of us are trying to concentrate."

Can you imagine what would happen to these people if they ever tried to live in New York City?

Picture the scene with subway vigilante Bernhard Goetz, leaning over and telling the gang of kids, "Look, I'm trying to memorize the new federal housing code, and I can't concentrate with you guys hanging around asking for money."

There is an incredible sense of order on the Washington Metro — no pushing, no shoving, no graffiti. A social deviant is someone who stands to the left on the escalator instead of to the right. There are signs, you see, and they're quite explicit. "Please stand to the right," they say. There is a system. It's all been worked out in an environmental impact study. People who want to hurry up or down the escalator are supposed to do so in the left lane, and people who want to stand have the right lane. And when this routine is disrupted, the crowd gets tense. They start tapping people on the shoulder; they squeeze between the left and right standers; they clear their throats sharply, shake their heads, and sigh a lot.

When someone's fare card gets caught in the electronic

gate, the offender is given the same treatment, and the thought running simultaneously through a hundred minds trying to hurry to the office is, "Tourist! Can't you manage your affairs a little better than this?"

Nobody is shoved. Nobody is cursed. Nobody is screamed at, but the energy behind the thought is put away and saved for the office and recess at the pool. It is poured into the all-night session, the marathon meeting, the report, the speech, the book. The answer to a gnawing gut is always to work harder, longer, faster, and better until there is no feeling because one's soul has been deposited chunk by chunk in the company store.

4

What This Town Needs
Is a Good Five-cent
Whoopee Cushion

GEORGE WASHINGTON was never known for his one-liners. He had lousy teeth and didn't smile much, and that more or less set the tone for the town that bears his name.

They haven't laughed here since Millard Fillmore was in the White House. They didn't really laugh much at him, either. They sort of smiled, but later, much later, after the rest of the country had started laughing and they knew it was safe.

Nothing frightens the good people of Washington quite so much as the unauthorized chuckle. Authorized chuckles are fine on formal occasions when the after-dinner speakers get up to talk or when Mark Russell sings funny songs or when one is reading Art Buchwald. But to laugh indiscriminately during the day, to guffaw at random on the bus or in the hall, to find the office or the report or the people in one's immediate purview hilarious is simply not done. Such behavior is considered dangerous and could be precedent setting. What if everyone did that? What if all the lawyers and congressional staff assistants and White House advisers and national reporters suddenly looked around and started laughing so hard they had to wee-wee?

Washington would close.

To protect themselves and the government of the United States of America against attack, they have developed a stone-faced deadpan that makes New Englanders look positively giddy. Go at them with a Groucho Marx nose, six hand buzzers, and an *ooga* horn, and they will not crack. They will direct you to a committee room.

When I first moved to Washington in 1982, a woman who had just left — fled is more like it — warned me that the place was completely devoid of yuks. "It's like *Invasion of the Body Snatchers*," she said. "I used to walk down the street and deliberately look people in the eye and smile. They didn't react. They can't deal with that kind of thing."

Back then I figured she was exaggerating. Now I think she was trying to break it to me gently.

The simplest attempt at exchanging whimsical pleasantries is met with a blank expression and matter-of-fact response designed to get the conversation back into federal mode as quickly as possible. I remember standing in line for stamps at the postal window in the Treasury Building. There was a sign on the counter that read, "This office has a limited amount of change" — which struck me as pretty darn funny. Since the line was long and nobody in it seemed particularly busy, I tapped the woman in front of me on the shoulder and said, "Don't you think it's ironic that they've got a limited amount of change in the Treasury Building?"

"No," she said, staring at me briefly and then turning back around to face the front of the line.

Just "no." Period. It sounded like a Bob and Ray routine. Bob says, "Well, Mr. Jones, would you like to show us around the laboratory and tell us a little about your invention?" And Ray says, "No." On radio it's a scream. In Washington it's business as usual. The woman in the post office line looked to be in her thirties, was well-dressed, and no doubt had a responsible job, maybe even in the Treasury Department. She probably knew all the regulations that would prevent U.S. Postal

Service employees from ever walking down the hall and getting change at a U.S. Treasury desk. She probably knew why the post office was short on coin and how it related to the dollar fluctuations overseas and the value of the yen. She had never stepped back from this close-range relationship with the facts to go on a wild, giggly trip into fantasy land before, and wasn't about to start now with some kook in a stamp line.

Laughter reveals a person's soul and makes him or her vulnerable — something to be avoided at all costs in a political environment. Washington is the town that invented the phrase "close to the vest." It also invented the vest. Take off the vest so you can get enough air in your lungs to yuk it up and somebody will make a fool of you, or try to steal the vest. So they keep tightly buttoned down here, ever on guard lest the enemy be preparing to tell a light bulb joke or send in the clowns.

On the day I moved into my apartment building, I encountered a woman who was at the barricades in the hallway. As the moving men were hefting a sofa bed into the living room and I stood there clutching a load of clothes, a suitcase, and a plant, the woman, with no expression in her voice or welcome in her eyes, asked, "Are you moving in?"

The question more or less put me away. After all, I was fresh off I-95 from Boston and didn't know any better.

"What was your first clue?" I asked her, laughing.

The woman looked slightly puzzled and said, "Well, I did see your things, but perhaps you're just visiting."

I laughed harder. "Just visiting." Ha ha ha. My new neighbor — Joan Rivers.

"Then you are moving in?" she said, fixing me with the eyes of a schoolteacher who wants no more nonsense and would like the question answered.

"Yes, ma'am," I said, realizing for the first time that I could be in big trouble in this new city. "I am indeed moving in."

"I see," she said, and continued down the hall.

I was in big trouble and still am. Even today, many years

and unfunny experiences later, knowing what to expect or not expect from the straight-faced Washington populace at large, the gears are not meshing in the great governmental mandala. A part of me clings desperately to the notion that this time, this one time, they will have to laugh because the situation is so totally ludicrous and, after all, they *are* breathing. At least, I think they are breathing.

As late in the game as the summer of 1985 I foolishly went for the funny bone with two strangers. The three of us were walking one behind the other through the underground parking garage leading into the apartment building. None of us spoke. We just kept opening the series of locked security doors and listening to our respective footsteps echo on the cement. Unable to stand it anymore, I turned to the guy behind me and said, "Do you get the feeling we're following each other?"

"No," said the crisp, unsmiling young man, who was carrying a briefcase and keeping his gaze somewhere above my head. "I'm just walking into the building and minding my own business."

Why do I do this to myself? Because I refuse to accept life without frivolity. I refuse to believe that the people who run our government and its peripheral industries want to be twisted sickies with no sunshine in their lives. All they need is a little help. Okay, a lot of help. So I keep trying to reach out, as the phone company says, and jab someone in the ribs with a well-placed elbow. It's a dirty job, but somebody's got to do it, and it does help preserve one's sanity after a day at the office.

That's where I started — at the office. Charity begins at home, and all that. I came to the *Boston Globe* Washington Bureau mistakenly thinking it would be a fun place. It had a reputation for being a bunch of wild and crazy guys who wore bizarre shoes and hung the telephones out the windows on slow days. Maybe there is truth to these stories, but you'll never prove it by me. When I joined them, they were about as funny as the John Hancock Mutual Life Insurance Company. We would march into our little cubicles in the morning, say very little to each other, and do our work until seven or eight or nine at night.

One day, to try to liven things up a bit, I stood in the hallway and screamed. I'd just had a telephone interview with Theodore Sorensen, the former adviser to President Kennedy, and it was terrible. I had asked a string of stupid questions, which were followed by terse, brilliant answers and long silences. After hanging up, I needed to vent and walked into the hall and let loose. Nothing primal or anything, just a good healthy blast, coupled with an explanatory note that went something like, "I just interviewed Ted Sorensen and made a complete fool of myself and hope I never have to talk to that man again!"

I figured we'd all have a couple of laughs, exchange terrible-interview stories over coffee, and then go back to work feeling that special glow people feel when they have traded some of their humanity with each other.

As I said, I was new. There was nary a rustle from the cubicles. Zip, *nada*, zilch, silence. A colleague did come out of his work area, brush past me to rip a story off the wire machine, and then walk back to his desk without looking up, but that was about it. You'd think his reporter's curiosity might have prompted a few questions like, "How terrible was this interview?" or "Do you scream in your hallways at home?" But he was impervious to attack.

I spent a year covering Capitol Hill with this man and never saw him laugh. At least never saw him laugh at whatever I was laughing it. He is truly one of the most brilliant, hardworking people I have ever known and has a sixth sense about Congress that is uncanny. He usually knows what they're going to do before they do it. I tried to learn the ropes from him but never locked in. Never even came close. The problem was basic philosophical differences: I thought Congress was a riot and he didn't. He'd get a kick out of some of the intricate maneuverings and power plays, but whenever he laughed,

I didn't get the punch line, and whenever I laughed, he looked as though he were in pain.

My first day on the Hill I sat next to him in the Senate press gallery watching a filibuster against school prayer legislation. Senator Daniel Patrick Moynihan stood on the floor, gesticulating vigorously to an empty room and quoting George Washington, which struck me as wildly weird and funny. I nudged my colleague and said, "Can you believe that turkey down there talking to himself?"

"Susan," he said, his eyes tired and sad, his shoulders sagging, "I knew you wouldn't understand Congress." Then he stood and left the gallery, presumably to vomit.

The Hill is one non-laugh after another.

How unfunny is it? Listen to this letter that went to members of Congress in the summer of 1985:

Dear Congressman or Senator,

I am teaching stand-up comedy at Open University in New York City. I am currently in Washington writing an anthology named *Humor on the Hill*. So far I am including submissions by Senators Goldwater, Hart, Kennedy, Bradley, Lott, Pepper and 79 other senators and congressmen. If you have not already submitted your favorite anecdote, true funny story, joke, etc., please do so at your earliest convenience. You may contact me by phone or mail your submissions to me. We plan to market the book nationwide, so show your constituents what a good sense of humor you have.

It's obvious why this guy is in academia instead of in Vegas. It's also obvious that he wrote his letter in Washington, probably with the help of a lawyer. This is what generally happens to funny people here. They die.

When I moved to Washington, a friend told me to be careful because terrible things can get to writers in the nation's capital.

"I know a humor writer who moved here from Minneapolis to do the light stuff for his paper," he said.

"What happened?" I asked.

"He got serious," said my friend. "In six months he was writing about the Defense Department."

Six months after coming to Washington, I was on the Hill writing about the MX missile. It's inevitable. It was a case of nerves. You look at your pathetic little feature idea after hearing members of the national press corps discuss the heavy issues of the day, and you need a news conference really bad. You want to be part of the good gray gang.

This stage passed, and I eventually found a place in left field where I belonged, but it was a tough transition. I still have to give myself pep talks every morning, look in the bathroom mirror and shout, "Okay, Trausch, you're going to go out there and laugh. You know it's funny. No matter what they tell you, it's funny, do you hear me, funny!"

God knows what the neighbors must think.

Very often I have to repeat the pep talk during the day, so formidable is the Washington wall of gloom that hits one like a monster beach wave and knocks one flat.

Getting into the House elevator one morning, I came up against one of the most dour human beings I had ever seen. He was a huge, grim-faced man in a tight suit jacket, and he was carrying a fat silver baton with a fat silver eagle on top of it. Huge, grim-faced men in tight suit jackets should never carry batons on elevators. He held it in front of him with both hands and looked sternly out above the eagle. It was too much.

"You waiting for a parade?" I asked, stepping into the car.

"This is the mace of the House of Representatives," he said solemnly, and I expected the people in the car to start humming "America the Beautiful." "The session does not begin until it is in place."

The place for the mace is a pedestal on the floor of the House, and it has been carried in there every morning Congress has met since 1841. Its origins date back to British parliamentary law, and it is supposed to be "presented," or held up, in front of anybody who gets out of line on the floor. It is not funny.

47

Neither are squeaking carts. During a Senate hearing in the Dirksen Building, a maintenance man walked down the hall outside a hearing room pushing a cart that was badly in need of oil. Its wheels made a loud, piercing squeal as he walked, and he walked very, very slowly. I kept looking around the room, thinking that surely someone else would start giggling uncontrollably, or at least shut the door. Nothing. It was like listening to the gears of government turning, but nobody seemed to notice.

Nobody ever notices. They have carefully cultivated tin ears that don't hear squeaking carts. I really believe that after a certain amount of time here part of the consciousness goes dead. The brain simply refuses to process what doesn't make sense, consequently shutting out half of what goes on in Washington.

I developed this theory in a take-out sandwich shop near the office. Walking in one lunch hour, I was bombarded by two radios blaring music from different stations on opposite sides of the room. On the hot-food side they had a Latin boom-chicka-boom-boom number, and on the iced-beverage side they had Barry Manilow singing "I Write the Songs." People in the shop seemed oblivious of them both.

"Doesn't that drive you crazy?" I asked the cashier on the Barry Manilow side of the room.

"Doesn't what drive me crazy?" she said.

"Hearing two radio stations at once," I said.

"Oh, no," she said. "I only listen to *my* radio."

That is the secret to survival in Washington. If people could hear all the stations at once they would collapse in a heap and never get anything done. But they are tuned to just one station — their own. Knock on their doors, rattle their windows, jump up and down in front of their faces, and they just keep humming along with that tune in their heads.

Working on a story about the junkets members of Congress take, I tried to contact the clerk on the Hill who keeps track of the trips and the costs.

"She's not here," said her assistant. "She's traveling."

"That's very funny," I said.

"What's funny?" she asked.

"Well, see, I asked for the person in charge of travel expenses, but she's not there because she's traveling," I explained.

"Oh."

Interviewing people for a story on how Congress deals with futuristic issues such as genetic engineering and robotics, I called the press aide for a representative on a science committee.

"We've got a book here about the future," the man said. "It came out five years ago."

"Great," I said, laughing.

"What do you mean?" he asked, not laughing.

"That's really funny — a book about the future that's five years old."

"Just what are you implying?" he growled.

"Nothing," I said. "It just sounded funny."

"Look, I normally get along with reporters, but if you insist on being difficult, there's nothing I can do."

I wanted to yell, "You can laugh, goddammit, you can laugh!" but he had hung up.

At a press conference in 1982 after the defeat of the Equal Rights Amendment, Eleanor Smeal, head of the National Organization for Women, criticized conservatives who said they had voted against the measure because they felt it would lead to unisex toilets. Smeal claimed they were merely using that issue as an excuse for killing the ERA.

"I don't think for a minute," she shouted, "that any congressman or state legislator voted on the toilet!"

There was not a smirk from the crowd. Nobody heard it. I was leaning against a wall about to sink to the floor in gut-busting agony, but reporters around me just kept taking notes.

Living in Washington, I have often felt the way I did as a kid at the dinner table with firm orders not to laugh. The adults sit you down in a chair that's too big and say, "Okay, now we're going to talk weird and slurp soup here for days, but you kids control yourselves." People in Washington think of themselves as mature, important adults in a big way. And mature, important adults are serious. You've probably noticed that the official portraits of U.S. presidents have never shown the man doubled up and pounding the vice president on the back. Sure, they all pepper their speeches with funny stories that somebody else wrote, but that's not the same thing. I want to know what makes this guy laugh when he's sitting at home on a Saturday afternoon. More important, does this guy laugh when he's sitting at home on a Saturday afternoon?

Politicians make a lot of noise about having a sense of humor, but for them the laughter is not casual fun and games. It is a tool, one more plate in the armor that keeps people at bay or in line or off guard. Senate Majority Leader Robert Dole engages in banter with reporters, and Massachusetts Representative Barney Frank is bitingly flip at hearings and the crowd goes wild. Yes, they make you laugh, but they also make you nervous about not keeping up or maybe becoming the butt of the joke. It's a power play rather than warmth.

That's why the armies of staff aides following top people around all day tend to be serious types who nod a lot. They're never sure whether they're supposed to be laughing or looking busy. Nodding gets them off the hook. It can go either way. If the boss cracks a joke that somebody else wrote, they can nod vigorously and appear to be chuckling. If the mood abruptly switches to a bad day at Black Rock, they can keep nodding and look grave.

I once saw four men in identical raincoats come out of the General Services Administration, cross F Street in lock step, and nod simultaneously as they walked. "Yes," said one. "That's right," said another. "Absolutely," said the third and fourth. I think they were staff people on their lunch break who forgot they had been turned loose for an hour and didn't have to do that on the street. But it's hard to escape the pervasive no-nonsense mood. It tends to sink into one's very bones from every angle and at every hour.

At the end of a long and particularly frustrating day, I hailed a cab on Pennsylvania Avenue and told the driver to take me home. I settled into the back seat and closed my eyes, glad that the battle was over.

It wasn't. When the driver pulled up to the first light, he turned around and said in a crisp Fuller-Brush-salesman voice, "Have you considered buying a cemetery plot in the D.C. area?"

"Give me a break!" I cried, holding my head with both hands.

"I'm serious," he said, slightly offended. "I sell them."

"I know you're serious," I said.

All the way home he talked plots, ignoring any attempt to lighten the conversation. "I know I look tired, but this is ridiculous" had no effect on him. Neither did "Can I be buried in Grant's tomb?" When I got out, he handed me his card and said, "You really ought to give this some thought. It's an excellent investment."

"Look," I said. "Doesn't it seem at all odd to you that you're trying to sell me a grave in a cab at nine-thirty at night? Doesn't it maybe seem strangely funny in a sick sort of way, kind of?"

"Not really," he said. "We're all going to die."

How do you fight this stuff?

After giving that question long and careful thought for the past several years, I've decided that the answer is whoopee cushions. Those little plastic pillows that make rude noises when people sit on them could bring new life to Washington. I'm thinking of a national campaign, with Americans sending the item by the thousands to their elected officials, bureaucrats, and news people with notes attached saying, "Start laughing or you're out of there."

At first the response is bound to be somewhat stiff. Politicians will no doubt make speeches about them and presidential advisers will formulate policy statements around them and very few people will sit on them. But as they get into the spirit of the thing and actually surprise themselves with a laugh or two right out loud in the middle of the working day, I'm convinced that humor can spread. The possibilities are endless. Imagine, for instance, State of the Union night with the entire government applauding the President and then preparing to sit down. Imagine the White House news conference with Sam Donaldson asking his three-part question and two-part follow-up, and then firmly and confidently sitting down. Imagine the ambassador of Romania toasting the ambassador of Brazil and then signaling all eight hundred diplomatic guests to sit down.

The whoopee cushion could change the seat of government forever. Who knows — as people get used to laughing spontaneously, they might even consider turning down their radios.

I think there are a lot of people in Washington who are dying for a good laugh — closet gigglers yearning to come out who simply don't know how to open the door. With the whoopee cushion campaign in full swing, I think they'd be ready for some sort of encounter group to bring them together. A committee would probably be the best vehicle for this, since everybody is used to those — a committee with an impressive acronym, like the Committee to Reform Attitudes Concerning Kidding and Uncontrolled Paroxysms (CRACKUP). It would tread delicately in the beginning, inviting members to meet secretly in private homes after dark with bags over their heads. They would sit around a table and take turns recalling funny things that had happened at work. They would bring memos and reports and newspaper articles and read them out loud. They would, of course, bring their whoopee cushions.

Guest speakers and entertainment should be brought in whenever possible, to indicate the bright spots on the Washington horizon where people have learned to laugh. Members of the Gridiron Club, Hexagon, and a group of satirical minstrels known as the Capitol Steps should be invited to do their thing and encourage people to come out from under the bags. Of course, Mark Russell and Art Buchwald should be there, as well as radio station WMAL's disk jockeys Bill Trumball and Chris Core, creators of the Gross National Parade, which brings madness to the streets of Washington every April. Government workers get dressed up in tasteless costumes for this event and parade through Georgetown. They form the Toro, Toro, Toro Precision Lawnmower Drill Team, the Synchronized Precision Briefcase Drill Team, the Tax Flashers, and the Wurst Band in Washington, which throws sausages at spectators. They give their names right out loud to the *Washington Post*, as Library of Congress worker Jane Coates did in 1985, and say things like "It just goes to show that under all those drab gray flannel suits beat the hearts of real reprobates." Inspiring, isn't it?

Unfortunately, the parade ends and these people go back to their jobs, but there is definitely the spark of possibility here. It needs to be fanned into a movement, and with enough whoopee cushions in the mail it just might. Nothing is hopeless. Human beings are, after all, human beings, and just because a town hasn't laughed much in two hundred years doesn't mean it can't start now. Let's not forget that if George Washington were around today, he'd have a great set of teeth.

5

The Most
Important City
in the World

THE REASON Washington has so much trouble laughing is
that it's carrying around an ego the size of the national debt.
People don't usually laugh when they're getting a hernia.

Ever wonder why all those folks in the nation's capital have
big briefcases? Ego overflow, that's why. They're hefting hu-
bris to work. It's part of the uniform. Even I carry a briefcase,
and I hate briefcases. Back in Boston I used to stuff the papers
in an envelope and walk out to the car. Here I have to put
them in ersatz leather with a shoulder strap and a zipper.

You're nothing in this town if your briefcase doesn't zip.
The really heavy hitters go for steel clasps and combination
locks. Some people carry two briefcases — one on the shoulder
and one in the hand. Other people have so many important
papers that they go to work in chauffeur-driven limousines and
have a team of assistants carry everything to their desks. The
President of the United States, of course, has the ultimate
briefcase — the black bag containing the code for blowing up
the planet. A military guard carries it for him wherever he
goes and sleeps outside his room with it at night.

The goal of all Washington professionals is to look as impressive with their briefcases as the presidential military guard
does with his. At the very least they want to look as though

they're taking a high-level impact study to a closed-door briefing, and that means a good, strong zipper. Even if they have only a peanut butter sandwich in there, they zip it up tight, walk briskly down the sidewalk, refuse to make eye contact with anyone, and frown. It's the federal way.

These people are suffering from the affliction that the rest of America assumes is merely an amusing little expression describing political ambition — Potomac Fever.

It lives, ladies and gentlemen, and it's as amusing as Godzilla. We're talking about a hard-core, bona fide quarantinable disease that is contracted through a virulent form of bacteria in the D.C. water supply. One sip of the stuff and you want to talk to Henry Kissinger. Drink too much and you start sounding like Henry Kissinger. The water acts directly on the nervous system, penetrating right to the very center of the ego, filling it with moxie and swelling it to the approximate size of Alaska. (The normal human ego is about the size of Pennsylvania.) That puffed-up look you see on the faces of people talking to you from Washington usually indicates that they have spent the day in a hearing room passing around a water pitcher.

Nobody has any kind of gathering here without water. It would be like a day without paperwork. Aides have built careers on bringing the extra water glass at the right moment and whisking away spillage before the television cameras see it. Those people huddling at panel tables, whispering intently in tight little groups, are usually talking about hauling in more water. They're also patting each other on the back and saying things like, "Golly, it sure is neat working in the most important city in the world."

Maybe you didn't know Washington was the most important city in the world. I certainly didn't until the clock radio clicked on one morning and an announcer's voice was speaking in the grave yet hopeful tones usually reserved for introducing the President of the United States. I turned up the volume, figuring the country might have gone to war.

It was a commercial.

"Riggs," the announcer was saying. "The most important bank in the most important city in the world."

It's hard to imagine that kind of hype anywhere else. "Cleveland Trust — the most important bank in the most important city in the world." People would be falling down in the streets. They'd also be taking their money to another bank. But in Washington the ad has been so popular that people have actually written in asking for recordings of the theme music. A local radio station did a feature on some of those folks who said the ad combined just the right amount of dignity and drive, and expressed the true essence of the nation's capital.

Can't argue with them there.

Ads for the bank are all over town. There is even one at National Airport that trumpets "Welcome to the most important city in the world" to people getting off their planes. I figure that's for anyone who may be harboring misconceptions about London, Athens, or Rome.

Other cities in the world have enormous egos, but none of them seems quite so obsessed with the matter. Paris, for instance, would not tout itself as "important." That would be considered déclassé. If one is important, one does not have to announce it. One simply is. Dallas — no shrinking violet in the "me first" department — chooses to talk of other things, such as down home barbecues and cattle and oil wells. Not even New York and Los Angeles push it, and they'll do anything for a buck. They tend to talk about how much fun they are, singing and dancing their way into our hearts with "Hooray for Hollywood" and "I Love New York."

But Washington doesn't want to sing and dance. That might endanger national security. Washington wants to be the most important city in the world, and its big problem in life, although it rarely, if ever, admits to this, is knowing that the world occasionally thinks of other things. Late at night in a dark corner of its power-mad little soul, Washington knows that somewhere west of the Potomac people actually go to sleep without caring if the pragmatists are losing ground to the hard-liners in the Oval Office. This is an anguished moment, and it is banished to the realm of the subconscious in the morning, buried in brisk walks with the briefcase, pompous pronouncements about duty to the American people, and gallons and gallons of water.

The reason people talk so much about their jobs here is that they need to assure themselves and anyone within earshot that they are indispensable to the survival of the free world. Conversation on the street sounds like the patter from so many Muhammad Alis, with people congratulating themselves and discussing their accomplishments the way people in other towns talk about the weather.

"I'm doing terrific stuff at Commerce," they say.

"I switched to the Hill," comes the reply. "Intelligence. The job was made for me."

"I knocked them cold with the proposal," says another authoritative voice. "No competition."

If the Washington Monument has always brought patriotic tears to your eyes, I'm sorry. It's really the national phallic symbol. Blunt and faceless, it stands as the supreme tribute to Washington self-absorption. Visible from every point of the compass, it towers over all it surveys and says with a touch of pique that anybody would need to be told, "I'm 555 feet tall and you're not."

The primary activity of the day is sizing up who's 555 feet tall and who's not. People look to the obelisk on the Mall, breathe deeply, and say to themselves, "Someday all that will be mine," or "Hot damn, you are looking good today, Jones."

I once waited for an elevator with a lawyer who stuck out his chin, slammed his right fist into his left hand, looked up at the ceiling, and said, "I'm really starting to track at the firm." We had one of those pass-in-the-hall-and-nod kind of relationships. I didn't care if he bought the firm and traded it for Green Stamps, but he'd obviously just hit the water fountain.

He was also trying to make his daily quota of prestige

points. Everybody here carries a score pad to keep track of the number of one-upmanship points earned in a twenty-four-hour period. The scoring runs as follows: two points for a straightforward "I'm good," which is what the lawyer had just won; five points for the more popular "I'm good and you're pathetic"; and ten points for the grand slam "I'm going to Camp David for the weekend," which can destroy an entire roomful of people with one shot. Any day that brings in fewer than fifty points is usually considered a waste.

There is a whole series of psychological war games that people play in the office to improve their point averages, and most of them are played on the telephone.

One of the most popular is "Breakaway," which, as its name implies, involves a person continually breaking away from a phone conversation without saying "excuse me" to talk to other, more important people. Phrases such as "Tell the senator I'll be right with him — this will only take a few seconds," and "Is the White House still on line two?" let the caller know exactly where he or she stands, which is to say, nowhere and minus five points.

The flip side of "Breakaway" is "Talk-over." In this one, two people of relatively equal rank keep talking at once, riding over each other's sentences and refusing to yield. When they hang up, neither knows what's been said, but each feels superior and puts five points down on the score pad. A lot of legislation is written this way.

"Telephone Tennis" is a game in which two people lob a call back and forth between offices, preferably for days, without having a conversation. The idea is to be the person who is called back and not the person who does the calling. You lose points when you call back because this indicates subservience. Return calls are made during lunch hours, early in the morning, and late at night to avoid finding the person in. This way, when the people involved do talk to each other, they can each say smugly, "Well, I tried to get you, but you were never at your desk." The scoring here increases for every day the game is played. Keep the match going for a week, making the other person return the call on Friday, and you get twenty-five points.

Some offices are so sensitive about call-backs that they have a flat-out "no return" policy. Calling the House Ethics Committee, I was told by a staff assistant, "I really don't have time to take messages. People here are much too busy to return calls."

"Three-Ring Roulette" is played by people who wish to appear too involved in their work to answer a phone on the first ring. So they allow it to go three times, letting callers know they're not sitting around waiting to pounce on the receiver even if that's exactly what they *are* doing. When they do answer, they sound rushed and talk about all the calls holding. These are the same people, by the way, who always have secretaries place their calls and who instruct them to say "Please hold for the State Department" instead of "Hello." For every call answered on the third ring a person gets three points. Five points are given for each call on hold.

"I Don't Do Windows" is an interoffice game played when the secretary is out and the phone rings. Everybody ignores the phone. Even if they're sitting around unwinding a paper clip, they ignore it. Whoever gets stuck answering the call takes his or her revenge by not writing down the message, or by writing it so illegibly that only a pharmacist can read it. I work with a man who feels it is an insult to his virility to take a phone message. "Someone called you today," he'll say, strolling casually by a colleague's desk. "I think it was from the FTC. I'm not sure." The whole tone is, "It probably wasn't important." Five points.

There are those in this city with egos of such Machiavellian proportions that they play something called "Fake-a-Phone," which requires an enormous amount of skill and cool. Disguising their voices, they dial their own offices from a pay phone and leave messages that the White House has called. When they return, the word has spread throughout the staff that the President is trying to reach them. They then must place a return call, usually dialing the National Weather Service or the time, and speak in hushed tones about matters of grave national concern.

"You're So Boring I Could Snore" is a technique designed to make the caller feel insignificant and unworthy of conversation with whoever is on the other end of the phone. An aide in Senator Ted Kennedy's office used to be quite good at this and would often yawn through the question as well as through his own answer. Asked about the closing of some federal offices in Boston, he gave a great groaning stretch and said sleepily, "I concentrate on national. This is my first and last experience with local issues." Three points.

An adjunct to the bored ploy is "You're So Stupid I Could Scream." Here the caller is made to feel like someone who doesn't know that the Capitol is the white building with the dome on it over on the big hill. Points are given according to quality of condescension on a scale of one to five. Very often the caller is also told to go read three months of *Congressional Records*, twelve reports, and an encyclopedia to become versed enough in the issues to ask intelligent questions. Two points are given for each pound of reference material on the required reading list.

An aide in Senator William Proxmire's office was able to win seventy-two points against me in a fast "You're So Stupid" match in 1985 and is undoubtedly the grand master of the game. Because he was so good, I took notes on the conversation — a move that probably hurt my score — and reproduce it for you here. (The Golden Fleece awards mentioned are the tongue-in-cheek recognition the senator gives to sponsors of overpriced government projects of dubious value.)

TRAUSCH: Could you send me your latest list of Golden Fleece awards? (*minus two, not assertive enough*)
PROXMIRE AIDE: Those were sent to the press weeks ago. (*three points; implication is, "But you obviously don't read your mail"*)

TRAUSCH: I'd like to know how the senator got involved in giving out this award and —

AIDE: (*three points for cutting in*) That's been written up many, many times. (*five points*) Let me send you a packet (*eight points*) of information and then if you still have questions (*five points; implication is that only a jerk would still have questions but that I probably will*) then you can give me a call. (*five points for lobbing call-back responsibility firmly into my court*)

TRAUSCH: And could you tell me if the senator looks at congressional junkets? (*minus five for not knowing what the senator looks at*)

AIDE: No, no, no. People expect us to do everything here. We can't do everything. We are one office for one senator. If you want to know about Senate junkets, you call the Senate Rules Committee. (*three points*)

TRAUSCH: And if I want to know about House junkets, do I call the House Rules Committee? (*minus five for admitting ignorance*)

AIDE: What you've got to understand is that the Senate and House are two separate bodies. The Senate Rules Committee is not the House Rules Committee. Are you aware of that? (*five points for speaking very slowly, as if talking to the family relative who has spells*)

TRAUSCH: Yes. (*minus two; never acknowledge the sarcastic question*) But are you saying that the Rules Committee in the Senate keeps the records for that body and the Rules Committee in the House keeps the records for that body?

AIDE: You're twisting what I'm saying. (*five points; throws the questioner off guard and elicits frustration*)

TRAUSCH: I am? (*minus five; total confusion*)

AIDE: You're trying to say that the Senate keeps track of trips and the House does not. (*five points; caller is beginning to sputter*)

TRAUSCH: No, I'm just asking if the Rules Committee in the House keeps track of trips the way the Rules Committee does in the Senate. (*minus three for playing into his hands and repeating this idiocy yet again*)

AIDE: I do not work in the House. I am in the Senate and work for Senator Proxmire. (*five points; caller begins to contemplate letter opener as a lethal weapon*)

TRAUSCH: (*grits teeth; minus five points*) I know you are in the Senate and work for Senator Proxmire because I called you there. What I am trying to find out is if in your travels on the Hill you happened to learn the procedure in the House as well as in the Senate. (*two points for a put-down, but too late to count at this stage of the game*)

AIDE: (*sighs; two points*) I don't usually get involved in these details. (*three points*) Let me check with one of our people who used to work there. (*puts caller on hold; five points*) Contact the House Administration Committee. Now I really have to run. I've got two other calls waiting. (*ten points*)

If I hadn't been there writing it down, I wouldn't believe it, either.

The Washington ego is a force of nature that is truly mind-boggling. And it doesn't confine itself to the office. It roams unchained in the night, intensifying with the evening's social activities and coming into full bloom at that decathlon of snubbery and snobbery, the Washington cocktail party.

Cocktail parties anywhere are bad, but here they are sadistic. The purpose of such gatherings is to bring as many egos as possible under one roof and turn them loose on each other. These functions are definitely not for the novice. Anyone who just likes to stand around and eat chip dip is dead meat. They'll see you coming and sharpen their nails on you as they're looking around the room for more substantial fare.

People at Washington cocktail parties are almost always looking around the room for something better than whatever they've got in front of them. If a group is clustered around a

House member when a senator arrives, the representative will find himself fanning the air with his endive sandwich in a matter of seconds. Likewise, the senator will be abandoned for the cabinet secretary, and the secretary for the top White House adviser. Of course, the representative, senator, cabinet secretary, and adviser are also doing their own scouting and abandoning, which gives these parties that special feeling of a panzer division on maneuvers.

When the daughter of a prominent congressman walked up and introduced herself, a friend and I were flattered until we realized that the area in which we were standing was practically empty, and she was between "hits." Her conversation with us lasted about thirty seconds. I had just asked her about her job at the State Department and she was in mid-answer when she stopped talking, snapped her head abruptly to the left, and focused on the door. There had been a sighting, and she was giving her full concentration to the timing of the attack. A couple of false starts, almost a wave, and then — "Congressman Scheuer! Oh, Congressman Scheuer!" She turned her back squarely to us and didn't acknowledge our existence for the rest of the evening.

"We've been trumped," said my friend, who advised me not to take it personally. He explained that this is how things are done. The congressman's daughter would have expected us to drop her in mid-sentence if we'd had the chance. She just got the chance first. Basic survival. Have a nice day.

The cocktail party insult is dropped almost casually. Sort of, "Oh, by the way, you're really not worth my time, but you must have known that." Or, as my friend says, "Here, hold my celery while I go talk to some important people."

Attending my first Washington party — a book signing — I met a woman who ended the conversation faster than the congressman's daughter.

"This party has such dull media people," she said, looking around and inching past me in the crowded room. "Last week I went to a publisher's party and met Daniel Schorr and Sally

Quinn." She paused, looked me up and down through her cigarette smoke, and said with a yawn, "What paper did you say you were with?"

"The *Boston Globe*," I said.

"Oh," she said, heading toward the bar, "I need a drink."

At my second Washington party a man efficiently licked chicken sauce from his fingers and said, as though the chicken was more interesting, "You know absolutely nothing about environmental politics. I'm surprised anyone would send you to Washington."

The reaction of the average schlep fresh in from the electorate is to find a banana cream pie and grind it into somebody's face. But they don't serve banana cream pies at Washington cocktail parties. They serve small stuff that pops easily into the mouth between zingers, which are tossed off with as little emotion as possible, except for maybe a tiny, frosty smile. The veterans can sail through these evenings of the long knives, giving as good as they get to the hostess who snubs them, to the lawyer from the competing firm deftly showing his scalps, and to the man from the State Department who says slyly, "It will be a cold winter in Moscow."

The rest of us should stay home and watch television.

Whenever I have tried for the witty comeback, I've landed on my nose. One time I thought I'd zinged a tax accountant at a Christmas party, but that was a terrible mistake. The tax accountant and his wife had spent a half hour or so explaining why they didn't like reporters. I'd listened for a while, but since it was Saturday night and the holiday season and all, figured maybe we could change the subject. Any attempt to do this was met with another anecdote of journalistic horror. Finally, I said to the husband, "So, tell me about your job."

"I deal with reporters a lot in my job," he said, "and it really bothers me the way they're so insensitive and always prying people for information that doesn't concern them."

"Right," I said. "Just like tax accountants bother me because they're always so boring."

64

I felt good for maybe fifteen seconds.

"I hardly think that was necessary," said his wife, thin-lipped, snapping a cracker in half.

"Really, if you can't take criticism you should be in another profession," said the husband.

They then went over to the hostess and told her I'd made trouble and started a general discussion about what the press should and shouldn't be able to give and take. I got a terrible headache and wanted a banana cream pie really bad. I was plainly out of my league.

It's not that the Washington press corps doesn't deserve a good going-over by a tax accountant or anybody else with a gripe. If egomania runs wild along the banks of the Potomac it's because members of the media have turned much of it loose. They not only nurture their own egos, which are immense, but they tend to everyone else's, bringing the messages of the most important people in the most important city to the most important news organizations in the world.

"Aren't you . . . ?" a well-known *Washington Post* reporter was asked by a writer from another paper who addressed her by name. In normal circles this would have been the beginning of a conversation, particularly since the two had met before.

"Yes," said the *Post* reporter, affirming her fame, ending the conversation, and walking away to more pressing matters, "I am."

A reporter walked into the office one day, shaking his head and looking as though he'd been to a summit meeting with the Soviets. "I just had a session with David Stockman," he said. Later I learned that he'd been over to the Office of Management and Budget for the regularly scheduled news conference with the public affairs guy and had picked up a press release. Stockman wasn't anywhere near the room.

But whatever you've got here you flaunt. Whether reporter, elected official, or bureaucrat, you've got to look a little better than you are. Life becomes one big cocktail party with everyone flashing his or her feathers to draw the attention of the big names coming in the door.

"I'm in the White House, so you'll have a lot of trouble getting in," said the man on the phone at the Property Review Board after we arranged an interview time. At the appointed hour I went to the press entrance of the White House and was met by puzzled guards.

"He's in the Old Executive Office Building," said one of the guards, pointing back down the street.

When I got to the man's office, I asked him why he'd said he was in the White House. He explained that his job was part of the executive branch and that he always referred to it as being "in the White House."

For all the sweat this country went through breaking away from King George, there is still a heck of a lot of lust for the throne around here. The capital of the free world likes to think of itself as a kind of royal court, and people are obsessed with how close they can get to the sun king. The State Department keeps something called "the order of precedence," or "the list," which is the seating chart for formal dinners listing everyone from the President on down in order of their importance. The order is not made public and is something every President can change around any way he wants, sending egos into euphoria and despair, depending on who is seated below the salt.

Congressional offices are run like fiefdoms or duchies, with the boss constantly being catered to, pampered, and followed by paper keepers, water bearers, and other minions. Members of Congress literally have traffic stopped for them on the streets around the Capitol when there is a vote, and have access to a whole load of congressional perks, including swimming pools, steam baths, saunas, whirlpools, and racquetball and basketball courts. They can have their cars gassed up and washed in congressional garages and get discount haircuts at special salons located in Hill office buildings.

Hair is very big here. Famous people's hairdressers are interviewed regularly, and legislative and presidential hair makes the papers when parts are changed or gray appears, or disappears.

During his bid for the 1984 Democratic presidential nomination, Senator Alan Cranston went home bald on a Friday and came back on Monday with very thin red hair and makeup. His ego consultants had obviously told him he needed to look younger and more tan if he expected to win the hearts and minds of the American people.

Better he should have just polished his head.

The debate continues to rage about Ronald Reagan's brown hair and whether he dyes it. I've seen him close-up at a press conference outside in the sun and can't tell what's going on up there. His barber, Milton Pitts, says nothing is going on, that it's all natural and that he cuts it every twelve days. The crowd went wild in 1982 when Reagan's slicked-back look became "fuller." There were before and after pictures in the *Post*, and the political analysts wondered if the President was becoming more relaxed in the job.

No hair has filled more lines of print than Kennedy hair. John F. Kennedy influenced a generation of barbers, and the phrase "Kennedy look-alike" still has them blow drying like crazy out there on the hustings.

Senator Gary Hart is one of them. Say what you will about Hart, but if the guy had looked like Dwight Eisenhower, America never would have added the word "yuppie" to its sociological lexicon.

Generally speaking, political hair is more elaborate in the Senate than it is in the House. There is a rough-and-tumble look to House hair, and the people in the south wing of the Capitol have bigger flakes of dandruff on their suits. On the Senate side they fuss more. Robert Byrd's blue pompadour is a work of art, as is Paula Hawkins's hair helmet.

I got my first Washington haircut from a man who cut Hill hair and embassy hair and, in a weak moment, had agreed to cut mine. Let's call him Paul, mainly because that was his name, and still is, for that matter. He was right out of the General Patton School of Charm.

Okay, hair people all over America have a reputation for being bizarre, but where else would you get a guy who treated the procedure like the invasion of Grenada?

"You probably came in here with your hair like that to test me," Paul said, slowly opening and closing his scissors as he studied the enormous task before him.

"I'm going to start with the sides and work my way through to the back," he said, taking a deep breath. "I want you to do as I say at all times. You will hold your head exactly where I place it. Do you understand?"

"Yes, sir," I said, telling him he could do anything he wanted as long as he made the back short.

"I can tell a lot about people from their hair," Paul said, ignoring me and pushing firmly against the side of my head. "You're the quiet type who spends a lot of time at home. Nothing dramatic."

Beautiful. For this I left Boston.

He finished an hour and a half later, and I hated it. He left the back long.

"I wanted the back short," I told him.

"Why?" he asked.

"Because I like the back short."

"You know what your problem is?" he said as he prepared to send a second platoon onto the beach. "You don't know what you want."

I knew what I wanted. But the closest thing to a banana cream pie in a beauty salon is the styling mousse, and I was afraid it might hurt somebody.

I should have known what I'd be in for in Washington from that first weekend visit back in the spring of 1982. I'd come to town to apartment hunt, and the real estate agent showing me around made Paul look humble.

"Washington is divided into two groups," she said. "The haves and the have-nots. I'm one of the haves. I've always gone to private schools — never, never, never to public schools — and I've had entrée to the right people. You won't get anywhere here unless you cultivate the right people."

I wanted a one-bedroom apartment, not a cabinet post.

I hadn't had much to do with real estate agents in other cities, but I did know they were generally into talking about closet space and making nice with the client. This one wanted to talk about Caspar Weinberger. She'd met him and called him "Cap." She showed me his street, told me where he took walks, ran down what other people in the administration thought of him, and carefully explained that I'd never be able to afford to live in his neighborhood.

A friend of mine from Massachusetts had gone with me on the apartment hunt and was sitting in the back seat of the real estate agent's car looking nauseated. She'd had abdominal surgery a few weeks before, but I could tell that more than the stitches was bothering her.

"Are you sure you want to move here?" she whispered through clenched teeth as the assistant secretary of defense walked ahead of us into an apartment building.

"We've got some punk kid here who thinks she's hot stuff," I told my friend. "Everybody in Washington isn't like this."

Ha! That was like General Custer telling the troops they'd fire a few rounds and be home for lunch.

6

The Word Factory

Words, words, words,
I'm so sick of words.
I get words all day through,
First from him, now from you —
Is that all you blighters can do?
— Eliza Doolittle,
My Fair Lady

WASHINGTON MAKES WORDS.

Where other cities have the fertilizer plant or the rubber industry or more artichoke farmers per square mile than any-place else in America, Washington has the open mouth.

Over a hundred billion words come out of the nation's capital each day. This is more than most big cities produce in a week and more than the entire state of Maine has manufactured since the end of the Ice Age.

The Washington climate is such that one word planted just about anywhere can grow into a filibuster. Dense, wild verbiage patches proliferate along the edge of the Potomac and are available to anyone in the D.C. area. They grow year-round and automatically replenish themselves as they are picked, reaching maturity in a matter of hours. Ripe verbiage is dry and fuzzy and usually stands about ten feet tall. Harvested primarily by congressional staff assistants, editors of the *Federal Register*, government lawyers, and political columnists, the verbiage is processed, minced, and fed to the American people at press conferences, cabinet meetings, agency staff meetings, luncheon speeches, high-level talks, medium-level talks, low-level talks, preliminary talks, briefings, background-ers, debates, panels, hearings, and closed-door sessions. It is distributed in form letters, statements, releases, legislation, news analyses, in-depth reports, magazines, books, documen-taries, and finally, weekend talk shows, which review every blessed word of the past seven days and send the viewing pub-lic deep into the TV listings looking for a *Star Trek* rerun.

If you think the voices of Washington sound bad when they come out of a television set in Minnesota a thousand miles away, imagine what it's like living with them. People in Min-nesota can turn off the set. Here they keep talking and talking and talking, and anybody stuck in a room with them has to keep listening, look interested, and make sense of what they're saying. When the Defense Department spokesman says, "We may have some words on that later today," a listener has to smile and say, "Thank you. That's very interesting."

They really do say, "We may have some words on that later today." Words are a commodity sent down the assembly line of the bureaucracy. Yes, we have no bananas this morning, but check with us later because a shipment is coming up from the verbiage patch. We will spend the afternoon whirling around in our cubicles and processing some for you. We will find just the right verbs for just the right nouns and serve it up in a sauce of modifiers that will seem filling but is totally lack-ing in substance. And it will sound like this:

"We must turn our attention to the logistics tail of spare parts acquisition as we fine-tune our initiatives and push them down to the operating level."

That came from Deputy Secretary of Defense William Howard Taft IV when he was asked what he intended to do about stopping his department from buying any more $400 hammers. It is vintage verbiage — authoritative, convoluted, and unintelligible to most of America.

Notice how the language avoids any mention of specific hu-man beings and attributes the action to the omnipotent "we," meaning everyone and no one, and making blame difficult should the words fall into the wrong hands. It also uses the verb "fine-tune," which creates the impression that what is going on here is a delicate operation instead of chaos. In addition, it leaves everything up in the air. We are turning our attention to fine tuning, but not saying when. Nothing has actually been fine-tuned yet, so if there is another $400 hammer in the garage tomorrow, it's not our fault. And if by some chance the general decides that this particular $400 hammer happens to be a good idea, we haven't fine-tuned so much that we can't take credit for it.

In verbiage circles this is what's known as having "wiggle room." A person can say one thing today, the complete opposite next week, but still use the same words to appear consistent. The phrase "cautious optimism" has about a mile of wiggle room on either side. So does "tentative acceptance" and "he is leaning in that direction."

People can straighten up from a lean in record time around here, and do. A strategic arms negotiator, Edward Rowny, did it in 1983 when news stories said he had criticized colleagues in a memo suggesting that they be replaced. Rowny told the *Washington Post* that the memo was "prepared for me" as "informal talking points" that "do not represent my views." Defense Secretary Caspar Weinberger bolstered his formerly leaning negotiator by saying, "I would like to know what is so sinister about this set of talking points."

"Talking points" are not words, you see. They are the stuff around which words may or may not be built. They are islands floating out there in the verbal sea, and a person can sail around them for a while, dock for a couple of nights, pick up whatever provisions are needed, and then move on, feeling free to wiggle whichever way the wind is blowing.

Even words that sound fairly forceful can be wiggled out of quite easily with the right inflection. In 1972 George McGovern maintained that he was behind Thomas Eagleton "one thousand percent" even as Eagleton was being removed from the vice presidential slot on the Democratic ticket. Usually, when anybody in Washington expresses an inordinate amount of confidence in a colleague, it means the ax is about to drop. Anne Burford had Ronald Reagan's "total confidence" during her turbulent reign as head of the Environmental Protection Agency, and presumably still has it.

After Reagan suggested opening talks with the Soviet Union in 1984, a *Washington Post* headline asked the musical question: "Reagan's Speech — a Momentary or Permanent Shift?" In the story White House aides explained the speech was both. They said the President was "opening a dialogue," but at the same time still standing tough against the Russians.

When Secretary of State George Shultz and Soviet Foreign Minister Andrei Gromyko met in Geneva in 1985, they spent days drafting a "communiqué" that said the problem of nuclear arms and space-based defense systems would be "resolved in their interrelationship."

A "communiqué," which should not be confused with "communicate," is a bunch of words that two foreign powers can live with because it says nothing and can be interpreted any way anyone wants to interpret it. Gromyko told reporters that the phrase meant Russia and the United States had to settle the space weapons issue before talking about anything else. Shultz said no, it meant that we'd all have to wait and see exactly what it meant.

So, if the big boys push the button, don't think of it as the end of the world — think of it as a resolution to those pesky nuclear interrelationships.

Verbiage is always devoid of emotion. It doesn't yell, "We're all gonna die!" It just hums along like white noise, smoothing everybody's humanity into a monotone.

Taxes become "revenue enhancers," so that nobody starts getting emotional about having to pay out more cash. When people have to pay out more cash, they usually get rid of the guy in Congress who voted to make them pay. Better for it to appear as though words, especially money words, have a life of their own. This is how the "Task Force on Entitlements, Uncontrollables, and Indexing" was born.

The deficit is never referred to as "our big fat dirty deficit," which would make the government sound irresponsible for not being able to balance its checkbook. The mess is not *our* deficit. It's *the* deficit, a hole in the ground created by God, or unforeseen economic variables, or the other political party. The deficit sits there by itself, "ballooning" and "burgeoning" like some strange breed of flora, perhaps a giant rubber plant. It has acquired a dignity in its independent vastness, and many have begun to consider it a pretty good shade tree.

No matter how badly the battle is going, the right verbiage puts a positive face on things. They don't even use the word "bad" here. They speak of "negative factors" or of something being "nonviable," but generally they make whatever's happening sound like a point for their side. In April 1985 when Congress voted down Ronald Reagan's proposal to provide more funding for the Nicaraguan rebels, presidential spokesman Larry Speakes refused to call it a defeat. "It's the beginning of victory," he told the *Washington Post*.

Certainly a phrase worth remembering the next time you lose your shirt in a poker game.

In 1985 House Speaker Thomas P. O'Neill messed up his introduction of British Prime Minister Margaret Thatcher to a joint session of Congress. O'Neill had presented Thatcher as "Prime Minister of the United Kingdom and Great Britain," leaving out the customary "and Northern Ireland." He did it because he had two people telling him what the proper introduction was, got confused, and blew it. But press secretaries don't get the big money to say the Speaker of the House blew it.

"These are not policy questions," his press aide, Christopher Matthews, told the *New York Times*. "They are purely procedural."

Way to go, Chris!

74

Matthews is also the guy who, after telling a reporter for the Quincy, Massachusetts, *Patriot Ledger* that the Speaker had nothing to say about the closing of the Quincy shipyard, explained that this should not be considered an evasive reply.

"I don't want to elevate this to the level of a 'no comment,'" Matthews said.

A "no comment" might sound negative and tick somebody off in Quincy, and that's another thing press secretaries don't get the big money for. The blunt edges must be polished, the point dulled, and the guts ripped out of the language.

Newly appointed Secretary of Education William J. Bennett could have inspired English classes across America with active verbs from Washington in 1985 when he was responding to criticism of his politics, but he, too, went into deep hum. Passing over colorful, memorable phrases such as "Balderdash!" or "Blow it out your ditty bag, Democrats," Bennett chose instead to say that the criticism directed at him was "counterfactual."

"Counterfactual" or "nonfactual" is a distant cousin to the word "inoperative," which means "it doesn't work anymore." But it should be noted that something can be inoperative without being counterfactual. Likewise, a counterfactual statement can operate very well in the right mouth. The word "inoperative," by the way, a holdover from the days of Watergate, is still very much with us. During my first summer in Washington, I had to call the gas company because the burners on the stove weren't working. When the repairman arrived, he asked gravely if I was "the woman with the inoperative oven." Not the broken oven or the kaput oven or the screwed-up oven, but the inoperative oven.

You hear this kind of talk everywhere. Two people were sitting on the subway and one said to the other, "I haven't made any vacation plans yet. The kids are being very nonspecific about where they want to go."

The kids probably speak English and can't communicate with their parents.

"Are you working press?" the gatekeepers ask at news conferences, and I always want to say, "Do I look like I'm on vacation here?" "Working press" — straight from the verbiage patch. Probably came up in the same crop with "intensive probe," "nuclear build-down," and "constructive engagement."

Official Washington is constitutionally incapable of writing punchy prose. In a March 20, 1985, article in the *Washington Post*, reporters Rick Atkinson and Fred Hiatt revealed that the Pentagon can't even give the specifications for a plastic whistle in less than sixteen single-spaced pages. A plastic whistle, for crying out loud. You pick it up and blow into it and it makes noise. But when the Pentagon orders them, they're called MIL-W-1053F's, and they must meet the following performance standards:

> The whistle shall be capable of emitting an audible characteristic sound when blown by the mouth with medium or high breath pressure. The center line of the air passage shall be tangent to the 13/32-inch radius for the solid construction whistle and to the 7/16-inch line radius for the split construction whistle of the inner chamber so that when the whistle is overblown, the ball shall continue to rotate and the whistle shall show no reduction or cessation in sound or marked change in pitch.
>
> Note: Overblown is defined as when the breath pressure is increased to maximum, as under excitement, so as to produce a higher pitch than the fundamental tone.

Overblown is right.

I think there is a fear in Washington that too much plain English will cheapen the place. People shape their vocabulary with an eye to the history books and the marble walls. The idea is to say something that will not get them in trouble now but will look good on the base of a statue, should posterity decide to pick it up.

"We have been tasked with enforcing security," said the sergeant at arms in the Capitol during an interview on increased vandalism and violence on the Hill. Back home in his kitchen he probably would have said, "If one more bomb goes off, the Congress will have my ass in a sling," but that wouldn't do for posterity. Just suppose this sergeant at arms was to have a monument built in his honor, and just suppose the monument committee was looking for the right inspirational quotation to carve into the stone and decided on, "If one more bomb goes off in the Capitol, the Congress will have my ass in a sling." How would that look next to the Gettysburg Address?

Lousy. There must be a resounding tone to the language at all times, and wherever possible, nouns must be turned into verbs.

"Task" in most parts of the country means "a job." A person performs a task and is never "tasked," which shouldn't be confused with "taxed," which a person is, a lot, but that's another story.

People in Washington have been tasking themselves for years, not to mention impacting, prioritizing, accessing, and absenting.

"I wish to inform my colleagues," said the senator after clearing his throat and asking for recognition from the chairman, "that soon I will have to absent myself and attend another meeting."

Not a bad quote for the monument committee, particularly if the statue will show the senator looking at his watch. Maybe they should have him dressed as Hamlet, considering how Shakespeare's character "absented" himself in the last act of the play before going to the big meeting in the sky. I don't think anybody has used the word that way since.

People usually absent themselves by leaving a room. One cannot call up the committee and say, "Hello, I'm going to absent myself today." That would be calling in sick, or "sickening" oneself. You can't absent yourself unless you're present.

Impacting and accessing, however, can be done by phone or through the mail, although being there generally gives one more clout. Systems are usually impacted — like wisdom teeth — and people are accessed. The phrase generally goes, "We're gaining access to Reagan and Bush." That means the accessors are communicating with the accessees, but not necessarily impacting administration policy. In other words, their objectives have been prioritized, nothing has been finalized, but with all those nouns turning into verbs people feel they must be getting somewhere.

The question is, Where? And will the English language survive the trip?

Probably not if it keeps traveling in the "high-occupancy-vehicle lane." That's what they call the car-pool lane on local expressways. It is designated by big "HOV-3" signs, which mean cars must have three or more people in them to be in that lane. Why three people in a car constitutes "high occupancy" is hard to figure. To me "high occupancy" would be four or five in a car, and three people, sort of "medium occupancy" — one more than two, which is nothing at all in occupancy circles unless you're driving a Corvette.

I always feel sorry for the poor slob from out of town who suddenly finds himself facing an "HOV-3" sign and isn't sure whether he's just wandered onto a landing strip for the Defense Department or onto the J. Edgar Hoover Memorial Highway.

Washington sign writers are bucking for posterity like everybody else around here, and they're not about to make things simple. That's why they put "No Left Turn — Crossing Situation" in the parking garage of my apartment building. It means that people coming into the garage shouldn't turn left because people coming out are turning right. In saner places on Earth this would be a plain old "No Left Turn" or a "Do Not Enter." It would not be a "situation," mainly because left turns aren't "situations." Lebanon is a "situation."

The sign writers have been working overtime in the D.C. Metro, too. "Priority Seating" is written in big black letters on seats near the doors of the trains, leaving a person to wonder who has the priority to do what. It is not until you read the small print underneath that you learn these seats are for elderly and disabled persons. But you can't read the small print unless you are sitting in the seat.

Reading the cryptic little message along the bottom of Metro maps produces even more confusion: "The alignment and terminus of the Green Line have not been finally determined."

So, has it been temporarily determined? Are the tracks crooked? Do you get on that baby and ride forever, like Charlie on the MTA? Is it better to take a taxi?

Washington likes to explain just enough to make people uptight but never enough to make sense.

When a man on the House Ethics Committee did not understand my question about financial reporting required for members of Congress, he said, "I am not following your fact pattern." Right away this stops a person cold. Did he mean that I wasn't making sense or that my facts were so tightly packed together that they required someone with more expertise to answer the question? When I had asked, I hadn't given a thought to the fact pattern but had just more or less let it rip. Could it be that I had created a work of art? Could I open a shop? "Trausch's Fact Patterns — $10 apiece."

I asked him what he meant by "fact pattern."

"Your interpretation of the information as you understand it," he said.

"But I don't understand it — that's why I'm calling you up," I said.

"That doesn't appear to be the case," he said.

"Are we communicating?" I asked.

"Possibly," he said.

Then there was the guy at the State Department whom I asked what America was spending to maintain troops in Beirut.

"Your question," he said, "is oblique."

"It is?" I asked, reaching for the dictionary, but I couldn't find "oblique" with one hand. I later learned that it means "indirect" and "not straightforward," but asking how much America was spending on troops in the Middle East didn't sound like a trick question to me.

I think what he probably meant was, "I don't know."

Very few people actually say the words "I don't know" out loud. Washington verbiage has been designed to gloss over ignorance and make everybody sound smart.

Members of Congress are so determined to sound brilliant that they allow themselves the privilege of "revising and extending" their remarks for the *Congressional Record*. That means they clean up their grammar, add flowery language, and otherwise make themselves look good in what is supposed to be an unvarnished chronicle of Congress at work. Periodically, people stand up and question the fairness of this, but nothing ever comes of the protests. In 1984 three members of the House sued to get the practice changed but didn't succeed. According to papers filed for the suit, one issue of the *Congressional Record* was amended so much that it showed ten thousand words spoken in ten minutes, which is impossible even by Washington standards. In 1985 Congress adopted the practice of using bullets, or small black dots, to indicate what was revised and extended in the text, but that didn't work because some members were having their speeches printed without the bullets. Congress then decided to print the afterthoughts in italics, which will work until somebody figures out how to get around that.

Most of what is said in Congress sounds like a foreign language and requires an interpreter. Legislators speak in the arcane tongue of the parliamentarian and refer to their number as "the leadership," "the whip," "the minority whip," and other kinky titles. Staff people speak of "my member," as in "My member is on Energy," or "Come over at noon and you'll be able to buttonhole a lot of members." Congress is a world of its own that becomes so entangled in vocabulary that people often have to work past midnight to figure out what they're doing.

In 1985 when Congress was voting on the budget, an explanatory note was posted in the Senate press gallery to help reporters understand the process. It was titled, "Possible Parliamentary Situation Part II," and read as follows:

Sen. Dole has offered a substitute to the budget resolution that only changes the reconciliation date to June 18, 1985. This is treated as the text of substitute to be inserted or an amendment that is amendable in two more degrees. The next step would be to offer a perfecting amendment to the substitute which is an amendment in the first degree and then an amendment which is an amendment in the second degree. He then offers a perfecting amendment to the text of the resolution proposed to be stricken by his first amendment and then an amendment to this perfecting amendment. This gives a total of five amendments pending with a total time limitation of seven hours.

The order for voting will be 1. amendment to the perfecting amendment to the resolution itself. 2. the perfecting amendment to the resolution itself. 3. the amendment to the perfecting amendment to the substitute. 4. the perfecting amendment to the substitute. 5. the substitute.

The time for quorum calls is counted against the overall time limitation on the resolution with the exception of quorum calls immediately before a record vote. The time for the vote itself is not counted in the 50 hours.

THIS ASSUMES THAT DOLE WILL BE RECOGNIZED EACH TIME TO OFFER AN AMENDMENT. THIS ALSO ASSUMES THAT NO ONE MAKES A MOTION TO RECOMMIT AFTER THE TIME ON THE FIRST AMENDMENT IS USED UP.

And if you think it's impossible to read, you should have been there trying to watch it.

Which reminds me of Representative Norman Dicks of Washington State, who had what was probably the best quote during the endless nuclear weapons freeze debate in the House in 1983.

"I have a parliamentary question," the Democrat said as his colleagues wound themselves into a verbal knot. "What business is before the House?"

Washington, D.C., needs to be rescued from its own tongue, but the people who try drown in semicolons. Alfred Kahn, head of the Civil Aeronautics Board in the Jimmy Carter administration, issued a war on words and demanded that bureaucrats start using declarative sentences. He came down particularly hard on overuse of the word "hopefully," as in "Hopefully, the legislation will pass," which he said was ungrammatical and ridiculous. He wanted active verbs and short paragraphs. He is no longer in government.

In 1985 Martha McSteen, Ronald Reagan's acting commissioner at the Social Security Administration, announced that she wanted her department to write letters that people could understand. A real rebel, this McSteen, and let's hope she doesn't go the way of Kahn.

The road will be hard if not impossible, and the *Washington Post* quoted McSteen aides as conceding that they had "a long way to go to clear away years of encrusted bureaucratic gobbledygook and obscure computerese." They expected that the process would take at least two years.

You don't just create a new form letter here and put it in the mail. There are layers within layers. This thing has roots. Charles Peters, editor of the *Washington Monthly*, keeps chopping away at it in his "memos of the month," but making fun of the stuff seems to have no effect either. Peters prints actual documents from federal agencies where spies risk their careers to get absurd governmental prose over to his magazine so it can be held up to public ridicule. But those memos continue to be written and that verbiage keeps on growing.

It is obviously invincible. Linguistic Astroturf it is, and it will never die. Or, as they say around here, "It is doubtful whether intensive analyses of the verbal system are impacting the structural character of the nomenclature in a non-positive capacity."

7

Hush-hush,
Buzz-buzz

SHHHH. If you're quiet you can hear it. A low humming sound like machinery in the basement or a hive of bees inside a wall. It vibrates through the marble and concrete of the federal city, tinkles the chandeliers in the great halls, pulses along the streets onto the expressways, and sends its indistinct mumble out across the country and around the world.

Listen. The click of a latch, the murmur of voices, the sliding of a folder across a polished table at midnight, the weighty clearing of throats. Secrets, secrets, secrets. Secrets being processed, being passed, being sucked from the very walls, being picked up as thoughts even before they are spoken. Shhhh. This is just between you and me, on the q.t., you never heard it here, don't quote me. Listen. What was that? Electricity crackling through the town as another rumor is born, making careers, breaking careers, skewing reality this way and that, on into history.

Shhhh. Listen. Do you hear it? It is the Washington rumor mill and it never sleeps.

At any time of the day or night, someone somewhere in the nation's capital is telling someone else something in strictest confidence while a bunch of people who weren't invited are speculating about what it is. This is usually happening on several levels at once, so that confidence sharers are speculating while speculators are sharing confidences, which explains why so many people in Washington are confused.

Say, for example, that Group A is meeting behind closed doors at the White House while Group B is caucusing on the Hill, Group C has locked itself inside a bunker at the Pentagon, and Group D is clustered around a water cooler at the EPA. The untrained observer might assume that Group D would do all the speculating while A, B, and C would tend to their own high-powered knitting.

Wrong, wrong, wrong. Group A is dying to know what's going on with Group B, and Group B spends half of its meeting talking about Group A, and all the groups would kill to get inside the bunker. The bunker, meanwhile, has prepared files on everyone else and is reading them out loud. Group D, while essentially speculatory in nature, has access to high-powered knitting of its own and could very well be discussing it in strictest confidence at this time, although no formal meeting has been called.

If you're wondering how people discuss matters in strictest confidence at a water cooler, they do it by holding those little paper cups up in front of their mouths as they talk. If there are no paper cups, they turn their backs to the room and huddle over the bubbler.

As Groups A, B, C, and D break up, they assure each other that they are mature, responsible adults who realize the necessity for keeping whatever they have just heard under wraps, out of the papers, away from the enemy, and otherwise locked up tighter than J. Edgar Hoover's grave.

In a matter of days it is all over town and headed for the *Donahue* show.

How does this happen? The way it happens in any small town, only more so. Each individual coming out of Groups A, B, C, and D passes the information along to a trusted aide, who passes it on to a few trusted friends, who give it to some trusted journalists, who tell their trusted editors, who put it on the front page of the paper for their trusted readers. As the story moves, confidences mix it up with speculations, creating the rumor-mill hybrid known as "confulations," or confusing and often contradictory facts. These give rise to more group meetings, more confidences, more speculations, more confulations, total chaos, and ultimately, the nomination of a candidate for President of the United States.

The big difference between Washington, D.C., and South Bend, Indiana, is that people there just relax and pass the dirt, while people here get neurotic about it. This is a city of schizoids who demand discretion in every office of public life even as they are trying to get their grubbies on the skinny and pass it around. Passing it around is how they keep their jobs.

What you've got to understand about Washington is that nobody really knows what's going on. Nobody. Not even the President, maybe especially not the President because they keep him on a pretty short leash and don't let him go to the water cooler by himself. His staff carefully controls what information he receives, tones down the confusion, and saves the juicy stuff for themselves and the press.

As Ronald Reagan once said, "I've had it up to my keister with these leaks!" Obviously, nobody told him when he took the job that he'd be working in a big white sieve overlooking a rose garden.

People talk so that they can get information. It's a trade. Since it's impossible to get a grip on the big picture, people spend their days negotiating for bits of the small one, which is not all that easy to get a grip on, either. Reality may be fairly constant in South Bend, Indiana, but it's a minute by minute deal in Washington. There are several hundred realities running around the track at once, continually shifting and blurring in and out of each other like the color fragments in a toy kaleidoscope. Whatever Groups A, B, C, and D think they have at any given moment can easily be something else in a couple of hours and then something else again tomorrow.

The talk must flow constantly and discreetly to keep one in touch, to allow one to test one's personal reality against the other realities, and to sniff the winds for a possible consensus so that one can be prepared to join it. If one has not been discreet and allows a reality that nobody else supports to be traced directly to one's door, things could go badly in the next election. At the same time, if one is too discreet and never lets anyone know how much one knows, things could go badly in the next election.

"I'll tell you mine if you tell me yours," people say, leaning together at corner tables of restaurants that have such names as Rumors, Whispers, The Intrigue, The White House Connection, and The Bottom Line.

There is much tippy-toeing around the pillars and the plants and exchanging of whispers in the hall. The higher up a person is, the more whisperers he or she will have at the left and right ear. Very often the whisperers have to line up and take numbers to get to an ear. While they're waiting, they whisper in each other's ears or meet with the whisperers belonging to the ears of other important people. A senior official and his or her attendant whisperers usually move through the city in a walking/whispering clump that looks very impressive in a committee room but has a hell of a time getting in and out of an elevator.

Interviewing a whisperer is a bit like talking to a double agent for the CIA. They don't just hand over the goodies. They have to make it clear how dangerous the mission is and how vital it is that their identity never be revealed.

"This is deep background only," an aide to Massachusetts Senator Edward Kennedy said when I asked him about some education legislation. "I don't want to be identified as a Kennedy aide or connected in any way with the committee. Are we clear on the ground rules?"

I told him we were clear on the ground rules even though I'm not too sure what "deep background" means and would be willing to bet that he isn't, either.

He cleared his throat and spoke in a lower voice. "I really don't know much about this and think you should be talking with other people."

I waited.

"That's about all I can tell you," he said.

"You're kidding," I said. "You put that on deep background?"

He wasn't kidding. Kennedy aides don't kid. They are on a mission from God, as are most people in the Senate.

The whole idea behind becoming a whispering aide — not to be confused with a whispering cypress — is that one will know things that other people want to know. Eventually, one thinks one knows so much that even saying nothing begins to sound like something.

"Is this on background?" asked an aide in the State Department. Her voice was soft enough to sound discreet, but loud enough so that anybody working near her would know that she had a call from someone who thought she was important enough to have information.

"Then let me go to my background phone," she said, sounding like Maxwell Smart, in the 1960s TV show, about to pick up his not-so-secret shoe phone.

One whispering aide went so far as to read classified documents on the subway to impress people with what he knew. Not the ultrasecret invisible-ink stuff certainly, but official enough to give a trainload of people a stiff neck and to get the *New York Times* interested. On April 21, 1985, the paper reported that "a bespectacled, middle-aged man" had been seen reading documents containing information about Reagan's upcoming economic summit in Bonn. The report, which ran, appropriately, on the newspaper's Washington Talk page, continued as follows:

His fellow riders, including a reporter, surreptitiously squinted at the five or six pages, which contained the sort of information that is normally classified. . . . Among other things, the squinters learned that Mr. Reagan will emphasize the need for lasting American friendship with the countries he visits and will solicit support for mutual defense arrangements.

Not exactly James Bond, but any crumb that drops in Paranoia City is considered major-league excitement. At least 75 percent of what's labeled "Secret" around here isn't and doesn't have to be, but believing that it is makes people feel a lot better about their jobs. Most Washington meetings could be held in the middle of the Mall and the world would pass them by, but calling them "high level" and locking them up in a room with a solid oak table gives them some class and gets the press jumping. Very often a government agency will send a fat packet of information over to a news organization with the word "Embargoed!" stamped all over it. That means it can't be released until a certain date, but the agency wants the press to have it early so that the people at the agency can flex their muscles and the reporters can get off on having secret stuff in the office.

Embargoes are usually broken, which makes everyone involved salivate even more. On the weekend before the President is scheduled to release the federal budget, copies are given to the media with all kinds of strictures about never breathing a word or a number of it until Monday, when "the embargo will be lifted."

The following warning was attached to a copy of the Defense Department budget:

This material may be broadcast or published ONLY after Secretary of Defense Caspar W. Weinberger starts testifying before the Senate Armed Services Committee, expected about 10 A.M. EST, Monday, February 4, 1985. It may move on wires no earlier than 7 A.M. that day and must carry the embargo notice to guard against premature use on the air or in print.

— Until release NONE of this material may be paraphrased, hinted at or alluded to in any way.

88

— This material must NOT be discussed with or provided to others who have not accepted the package on an embargoed basis.

— In advance of release, NO telephone inquiries on this material will be accepted by Defense Department personnel. Correspondents must ask their questions in person and must acknowledge acceptance of the embargo by showing OASD/PA officers this embargo sheet.

And if that wasn't enough, press officer Jack Powers called from the Pentagon with a verbal warning.

"Do you understand that under no circumstances are you to release this information before Monday?" Powers sounded as if Dark Forces were already gathering on the horizon.

"I did get that impression," I said, explaining that I never wrote about the Pentagon and didn't want to.

"I'm very serious about this," he said. "I will hold you personally responsible if this appears in your newspaper."

"What does that mean?" I asked.

"Do I have your word that absolutely no part of this budget will appear in your paper?"

"Mr. Powers," I said. "If I break this embargo you get my first-born son."

"How do you spell your last name?" he asked.

Of course, the *Globe* broke the embargo along with every other newspaper, and I can only hope that if I have children someday, they will be girls.

The rumor mill was working overtime that weekend and got word around town that the *Post* was going with the budget story in Monday morning's paper. Never mind that the *Times* had gone with it on Saturday and that most papers had already written about it to death for weeks. This was budget weekend, an embargo had been imposed and broken, Jack Powers was abroad in the land making pacts like some modern-day Rumpelstiltskin, and Washington was positively dizzy for having so much to do.

It's never been entirely clear whether the unstable nature of Washington life creates rumors or whether the rumor mill creates Washington. Did the *Post's* honchos wake up on Sunday morning solid in their decision to get out there and break an embargo, or did the buzzing make them do it? When Groups A, B, C, and D go forth into the day with their respective hot ones, are they passing along news or making it? The only thing anybody knows for sure is that if the rumor mill ever shuts down, the government wouldn't be able to function.

Washington rumors come in four basic styles: the Leak, the Growing Perception, the Hoot, and the Grosso Profondo.

Leaks, as President Reagan has observed, are the most common, and there are hundreds of them a week. A leak is information trickling from the inside to the outside and is usually news-oriented, although leaks do occasionally go the other way. There are leaks about the Middle East, the arms talks, or the budget compromise. They come from "highly placed sources" and "observers close to the President." Very often policy makers will leak a biggie about themselves or a decision they are about to make to see what kind of reaction it gets. This is called a "trial-balloon leak." If they hear Bronx cheers, the plan will be denounced as "pure speculation" and dropped behind a file cabinet. If it is considered brilliant, they will say that they've been pushing it for years but no one listened.

The Growing Perception is something that forms over time. If there are enough leaks about a particular subject, a perception may begin to take shape. The perception is never set in cement but pulsates, sometimes expanding, sometimes contracting. A more accurate name for it would be "the growing-shrinking perception" because it can go either way, although it never disappears entirely or inflates to the point where it becomes a Grosso Profondo. The Growing Perception usually concerns people's job performance and how well or how poorly or how disappointingly middle-of-the-road they are doing. It also covers the position of the United States in the world, the inflationary spiral, and the metric system. It is not an exciting rumor but a serviceable one, particularly for people who spend a lot of time in think tanks.

The Hoot is a kick in the pants. It is the one that makes the cocktail party sizzle and the lunch table hum. It is based on fact, as most rumors are, but the fact is so wild or silly or risqué that it invites embellishment and is usually associated with the person for the rest of his or her life. Some of the great Hoots of recent history have been Wilbur Mills and Fanne Fox; Elizabeth Ray and Representative Wayne Hays; Gerry Ford's Polish interpreter, who said America lusted after the Polish people; Michael Reagan's rift with his stepmother, Nancy; James Watt and the Beach Boys; and Billy Carter. Watt's and Carter's rumors eventually became Grosso Profondos because of a long series of Hoots — and in Carter's case, charges of influence peddling with Libya.

In 1981 Vice President George Bush was also involved in a Hoot that nearly turned into a Grosso even though none of it was true. It was one of those hyper times for the rumor mill — the first few months of a new administration. The town goes crazy with new administrations, having thoroughly gossiped itself out during the past four years with the old one. The prospect of new people, policies, and peccadilloes is almost too much, which is exactly what the Bush rumor turned out to be.

It circulated for several weeks and was the subject of an in-depth *Washington Post* analysis headlined, "Anatomy of a Washington Rumor." Interestingly enough, it was co-written by Janet Cooke, the reporter who had to return a Pulitzer Prize because her entry was more fiction than fact.

According to the *Post*, the whole thing started with a car accident on Capitol Hill that didn't involve Bush or anybody else in the administration but did bring people out into the street to see what had happened. At the time a policeman told a woman acquaintance standing on the curb that he'd heard the vice president had been shot elsewhere in the city that night.

The woman went back to her apartment and called TV and radio stations to find out if they had the story. Nobody knew anything about the vice president getting shot — mainly because the story was off the wall — but everybody started investigating it. The investigation fed the mill and the mill fed the investigation until the story circulating around Washington became: George Bush had been shot after leaving some woman's Capitol Hill apartment late at night, and was consequently being investigated by the FBI. The major dailies were looking into it, Jack Anderson was on the scent, and TV crews were staking out the woman's apartment.

The rumor eventually died, but it was kept alive with tubes and respirators long after the vital signs were gone. Just writing about it one more time will probably get a few more twitches out of the bones. People are loath to let go of one like this because of its obvious Watergate potential. Tied to the White House, loaded with the prospect of high crimes and misdemeanors, it evokes memories of that wonderful wickedness that once had America collectively glued to its TV screens and focused on Washington every night of the week.

Watergate was the granddaddy of all Grosso Profondos, which is a type of rumor so vast and so deep that it practically chokes the mill. A Grosso Profondo is like the finale of a fireworks display on the Fourth of July and sends everything up in the air at once — Leaks, Hoots, Growing Perceptions, confulations, whistles, and bells. Although it is more than a decade old, the Watergate Grosso is still very much with us, and the town continues to whisper about who Deep Throat may have been and what the President knew and when he knew it. In a lot of ways Watergate is treasured because it justified the existence of the rumor mill. Looking at the scandal in all its sleazy vastness, people can pat themselves on the back and say, "Thank God none of us can keep our mouths shut in Washington or Richard Nixon would still be in the Oval Office."

Notice that just about every scandal since has had the word "gate" on the end of it — Billygate, Koreagate, Debategate. What I'm waiting for is a sizzler in a guard post at one of the entrances to the White House grounds, which will no doubt go down in history as "Gategate."

There is a real nostalgia for Watergate memorabilia, as was evident on June 16, 1982, when both Democratic and Republican groups held tenth anniversary parties in remembrance of the break-in. Black crepe paper festooned hotel suites, and at one party name tags were made with masking tape, symbolic of the tape used to hold open the door latch of Democratic party headquarters in the Watergate Hotel. Groups rented rooms in the Howard Johnson's across the street from the Watergate so they could stand on balconies, cocktails in hand, and stare over at the place where it all happened. People were fighting over the booking of Howard Johnson's room 723, which was the very room where E. Howard Hunt and his crew had hunkered down over the monitoring equipment. Edward Zuckerman, who was sponsoring a Watergate anniversary fund-raising party for Indiana Representative Floyd Fithian, had mistakenly booked room 419 because he'd read about it in William Manchester's book *The Glory and the Dream.*

"I booked it months in advance and was really proud of myself," a dejected Zuckerman said in an interview that night. "Then the desk clerk said to me, 'Why do you want that room anyway? Nothing happened in there.'"

A CBS crew had room 723, and Austin Ruse of *American Film* magazine had room 710. Nothing at all happened in room 710, but it was supposed to that evening if Frank Wills showed up for the party. Wills was the janitor in the Watergate who spotted the masking tape on the office doors and called the police.

"We're the only party that got Frank Wills," said Ruse. "It's just that he's not here — he's in Texas." Minus the guest of honor, Ruse said he had other excitement planned and whispered that he was going to call the police to raid his own party if they didn't arrive on their own. No Watergate party would be complete without the police, he reasoned, and the visit would get him mentioned in the gossip columns the next day.

Watergate Liquors, located in the basement of the hotel, filled its windows with bottles of its own brands that picture the hotel on the label. The store did a brisk souvenir trade that night and still does, not only with the liquor but with gift items such as "Watergate Bug Juice," and T-shirts and cloth bags imprinted with Nixon's face.

James Herrald, former chief engineer and superintendent for the Watergate, is selling a souvenir of his own — the original lock that the burglars picked to get into room 600. He wants $10,000 for it. So far no takers, but stay tuned. The hotel still gets a steady stream of visitors inquiring about suite 600 and asking to see it.

Whitaker Brothers Business Machines across town on Georgia Avenue also gets its share of gawkers who want to see the Shredmaster Conveyor 400 that Nixon's Committee to Re-elect the President (CREEP) used to chop up memos. The company's founder, James Whitaker, took it back when the Nixon people felt it was giving them a bad name. He keeps it on display in his show room, can quote from the hearings, and has an extensive Watergate scrapbook.

The shredder, despite Richard Nixon, or maybe because of him, has become very much a way of Washington life. Robert Scott Church, public affairs officer for the Defense General Supply Center, which purchases shredders for all government offices, said it would be impossible to estimate how many there are.

"Probably millions," he said.

That's because the secrets that aren't whispered into the Washington wind are stacked high in paper mountains marked "Eyes Only," "Confidential," "Secret," and "Top Secret." When it's time for these documents to die, they cannot be pitched willy-nilly into the nearest wastebasket. They must be shredded, pulverized, disintegrated, burned, chemically dissolved, or otherwise killed dead so that they can never talk. This stuff is so secret that some agencies won't even talk about how they destroy it.

"We wouldn't respond to that," said a spokesman for the CIA when asked what it does with waste paper. The Defense Department didn't want to discuss it either, and sent over a book titled *Information Security Program Regulation,* which had been "issued under the authority of DOD Directive 5200.1" and outlined "Disposal and Destruction" in chapter 9.

One person in the Defense Department who does speak English in addition to being about the only guy there with a sense of humor is Army Major William Tobin, who has figured out a way to trade on this supersecret mania. After spending months getting the proper clearance, Tobin started his own business: stuffing shreds of secret documents into little Lucite boxes and selling them for $3.95 a throw retail and $6 mail order. He hauls the shreds home in garbage bags and assembles his "Secret Souvenirs of Washington" at his kitchen table. Each box comes with an authorizing signature certifying that the paper is, or was, an official secret of the U.S. government.

Tobin has been getting orders from all over the country and says that one of the best sales spots is in the gift shop in the Pentagon and that military people are some of his best customers.

Proving once again that a Washington secret is irresistible, even if it's dead.

Some military folk have so many secrets to keep that they're beginning to lose track of them. According to an April 2, 1985, *New York Times* story by Richard Halloran, the Defense Department has 1.2 million documents classified as Top Secret, and many of them get that label automatically, regardless of their content. Halloran noted that the air force inadvertently listed a secret aircraft in its 1986 budget. He also reported that Caspar Weinberger, warming to a speech on the dangers of exporting U.S. technological know-how overseas, said right out loud and not anywhere near deep background that the Soviet Union used this technology to place listening devices near a submarine base. Until then, U.S. knowledge of the listening devices had been classified as Secret.

Again I see Maxwell Smart on the shoe phone. He dials headquarters and says crisply, "Would you believe we think it's a soft-rock radio station?"

The commander in chief with the leaks up to his keister can't keep his mouth shut either. In July 1982, as the White House was carefully not telling anybody that Murray L. Weidenbaum, chairman of the Council of Economic Advisers, had submitted his resignation, Reagan accidentally let it slip in St. Louis.

"I goofed," Reagan said, much to his credit.

Washington simply has too much to hide, pass around, and find out to be able to keep these categories straight. The strain is becoming unbearable in many quarters. The National Security Agency, for instance, is so uptight that it won't identify itself when its phone rings. Call the kings of electronic surveillance and say, "Hello, NSA?" and they'll say, "What extension did you want?" Ask again, "Is this the NSA?" and there is silence. No doubt they tap all their own lines and have warned themselves time and time again that loose lips sink ships.

I know a couple of people there who are not allowed to identify where they work. They can say only that they "work for the government," which is a little like living in Detroit and saying, "I'm in cars." It just invites more questions, like "What do you do for the government?" and "Why can't you say?" and "Would you like me to speak directly into your tie clip?"

If you don't believe that people speak into tie clips, you've never been to the Counterspy Shop on Eighteenth and K streets. They have a sign over the door and everything. This is your basic, down-home retail supermarket for spooks, and they're serious. (Who isn't serious in Washington?)

The Counterspy people can sell you anything from a simple wiretap to a bullet-proof Mercedes. Walk in, look around, and pick up a cigarette lighter–camera for the office or a bomb sensor for the car or a couple of debugging devices or a deluxe "countermeasure kit" for every occasion. Not the sort of thing you'd find in your local shopping mall, but here it is considered as essential as the hardware store. After all, this is the town where secrets float in the air like pollen. Without the right equipment that stuff can very easily get away from you, or sneak up on you, or just plain fly up your nose.

No doubt about it, Washington can make a person uptight. It's gotten to me on occasion. During the spring of 1985 as I was working on this book, I heard a noise outside my bedroom window and looked out and saw a long wire banging against the screen. Walking onto the balcony to study the situation, I noticed that the wire extended from the window of another apartment several floors up. There was what looked like a black button on the end of the wire. Was it merely a stray TV antenna, I wondered, or was it a microphone? Was it an innocent coincidence or the beginning of a Big Brother nightmare in which sophisticated recording devices would pick up impulses from my word processor and turn me over to the state? Should I go upstairs, knock on a door, and indicate that I know what is happening or ignore the whole thing and act casual?

Standing on a balcony actually giving nodding acknowledgment to these thoughts that never would have occurred to me in a garden apartment in Hingham, Massachusetts, I saw how deeply Washington could sink into one's psyche and realized that I was probably warped for life. Thinking back on what I did about the wire, I'm convinced of it. I decided to monitor the thing — the very word that came to mind at the time was "monitor." Peering out from a slat in the venetian blinds, I would watch the wire sway back and forth, thinking that maybe the wind activated an infrared camera or a highly sophisticated listening device that someone had purchased at Eighteenth and K. Standing on the balcony pretending to busy myself with the porch furniture, I would follow it out of the corner of my eye, reasoning that the wire seemed inordinately long for a TV hookup and that the spies, whoever they were, had left it hanging because they figured anything so obvious would not be suspect.

For two weeks I monitored the wire and discovered that what it mostly did was bang against the screen. Then one morning it was gone, leaving me to wonder, as I still wonder and will always wonder, why, and what if, and who, and when, and what happened to the information they got, if they got any, and especially, what did the rumor mill do with it, for how long, and did anybody care?

8

Hildy Johnson
Is Dead and Gone
and Living in D.C.

"I WANT A PERPETRATOR, a weapon, and a dead body,"
the reporter said, crumpling up a press release and flinging it
into the wastebasket.

She had done the police beat back home and was now covering Congress. She had just returned from a Washington-
style "stakeout" and was feeling homesick for an old-fashioned
homicide. Washington journalism can do that to you.

The reporter had come to the capital as all of us in the
fourth estate come to the capital — deluded. Washington
looms like Mount Olympus on the horizons of a thousand
city rooms, and we feel we must go to test our mettle and
write brilliant, penetrating prose about the pressing events
of our time. Then we get here and find out nothing much is
going on.

This is a downer that nobody wants to acknowledge, so we
write a lot. Standing there with our notebooks and pens, not
to mention the going-away gifts from the gang back home,
it's just about impossible to look the nonevent in the eye and
write: "WASHINGTON — Nothing much happened in the nation's capital today, so why don't you people go read the
sports pages."

Instead we write: "WASHINGTON — Highly placed sources in the White House and Congress have indicated that they are 'deeply concerned' about the events of the past several days and will be 'considering possible alternatives' to the present course should the situation continue."

The idea is to report the news as though the weight of it could shift the Earth right off its axis and into a black hole. If you're in television, you do this by looking concerned and lowering the voice several octaves. If you're in print journalism, you make sure the first paragraph of the story is at least five lines long and impenetrable. Ending it with a question mark helps, as the *Washington Post* did in this January 1984 interrogative:

> Has President Ronald Reagan really changed his approach to dealing with the Soviet Union or was the more positive tone of yesterday's speech — in sharp contrast to Reagan's previous portrait of the USSR as the "evil empire" — a temporary, election-year detour from the visceral long-standing combativeness toward Moscow?

Rattle that one off at your next barbecue and watch the back yard clear out.

In February 1985 the *New York Times* anesthetized readers with this one:

> White House aides and Republican advisers concede that the plethora of seemingly urgent issues that arise and briefly disappear mark a striking change from Mr. Reagan's first term when he showed, in his first 100 days, that he was determined to change the tides of history. Instead, Mr. Reagan's second term seems to be marked by shifting currents.

And from the *Boston Globe* in November 1983:

> In its first debate on a nuclear weapons freeze, the senate last night voted to table the measure and instead endorsed a more moderate build-down proposal. Neither vote represented

final action, but in a test of strength supporters of the build-down were in the clear majority despite criticism from liberals that the proposal amounted to a "general's dream" rather than arms control.

That was my story and I have no idea what I was talking about. Anybody who knows what I was talking about, please call. On second thought, forget it. I don't want to know.

It was obviously another one of those embellished nuances. That's what we do here — embellish nuances and track twitches. We're a lot like researchers who have stared too long through a microscope lens at a field of amoebas. Something moves across the field and we have an attack. We jump up and down, shout "Peril in divided Congress!" and want to stop the presses. It's not that we're trying to dupe America. It's just that we have become so nearsighted that we really believe something dramatic can happen in Washington.

The mere possibility of drama is enough to send the troops into a frenzy. On June 3, 1985, the *Washington Post* reported the following under the headline "Weinberger, Shultz Clash Due on Pact":

Defense Secretary Caspar W. Weinberger and Secretary of State George P. Shultz are expected to clash today at a closed National Security Council meeting called to discuss ways to handle expiration of the SALT II control agreement at the end of this year, according to informed sources.

Now, a confrontation between Weinberger and Shultz is not something you'd want to spend a lot of money on to get a good seat to watch. It's more like a board meeting. A "clash" for these guys would be their saying, "You know where I stand — it's in my memo" or, maybe, "Hrrrumph." They don't even take off their suit jackets. But to the action-starved Washington reporter it is the equivalent of gang warfare.

This myth about members of the national press corps leading exciting lives was started by a group of reporters who had been standing at a stakeout too long without food.

The Washington stakeout is about as exciting as waiting for a bus. Actually, it's more like waiting for Godot. When you wait for a bus, you eventually go somewhere. What happens at a stakeout is that a bunch of politicians go into a room for a secret meeting and stay there for several hours doing whatever it is politicians do in secret meetings — play Monopoly, practice the secret handshake, show slides from their latest fact-finding mission to Bermuda, who knows?

Then they come out, usually one by one or in coy little clusters, and look surprised that reporters have been standing around outside waiting for somebody to hand them a story. The reporters have been standing around outside waiting for somebody to hand them a story because the aides to the coy little clusters of politicians have announced the event hours and sometimes days in advance, giving time and place, telling the press where to stand and where to set up the microphones and cameras.

"There will be a stakeout," the aides say, meaning there is no scheduled press conference but reporters can ask the politicians questions as they emerge from the locked room, which means there really is a press conference but the politicians don't want to look as though they're seeking publicity because that might shoot their credibility as secret-meeting holders.

When you see this fiasco on the evening news, you think, "Good Lord, look at those important people being attacked by those hard-hitting, aggressive reporters defending the public's right to know down there in Washington — this must be big!"

Relax. When the people come out of the room, that's a good time to go get a beer so you won't have to run into the kitchen during the weather report.

My friend the former police reporter with the crumpled news release had been staking out a meeting of Democratic senators who were re-electing Robert Byrd as their minority leader.

Everybody out there in the real world who stays awake

nights thinking about Senate minority leaders raise your hand.

Good. This crowd has taste.

Washington loves to think about Senate minority leaders and thought about this particular election for weeks, months, even years in advance. When the day finally arrived in December 1984, the press had whipped itself into an anticipatory froth. There were stories about Lawton Chiles's challenge to Byrd's seat and about how this signified the rise of the Young Turks against the old guard as well as sweeping institutional change and a great ideological Sturm und Drang in the Senate of the United States of America. People stood in stakeout groups speculating on the impact the election would have in years to come, taking notes on each other's theories, and generally looking as though someone had died or was about to.

Then the votes were cast, and Byrd won 35 to 11, and the matter vanished in a cloud of blue smoke. Another colony of amoebas took the field, and the press corps marched in lock step to cover the next crisis that none of us can remember now. That's how priorities are set and passions dictated around here. Events snap in and out of focus like some kind of disjointed slide show. *Click-click*, minority leaders; *click-click*, the budget; *click-click*, the White House staff; *click-click*, the arms talks; *click-click*, the Pentagon; *click-click*, Central America.

Doors open, people come out. Doors shut, press releases come out and fill the rows and rows of bins in the press galleries. People speak, the words run together and make no sense. Nothing feels grounded, and packs of reporters keep running down hallways after the story they're really not sure is there but better get because everybody else is writing it.

I remember running with the pack at midnight, down two floors from the House press gallery to a news conference where the whole assemblage of camera crews and scribblers acted as though it were two o'clock in the afternoon. Running back upstairs with about ten minutes to write the story, I listened to the echo of the footsteps in the dimly lit, shadowy halls, looked up at the enormous statues of famous people from the past who seemed to be either frowning in disapproval or about to smirk, and wondered why I wasn't asleep — or if I was.

New to the Hill, I once raced with a group of reporters to corner some senators who had come out of a secret meeting on the MX missile. Dodging elbows, jumping TV cables, I wedged into a strategic piece of ground between a three-hundred-pound cameraman and a pillar, and started to write.

Words — fired from disembodied voices somewhere up front in the circle of hot lights — began hitting the notebook like buckshot: "The American people . . . the time has come . . . the most pressing issues facing our nation to-day . . ." I strained to catch the words, leaned hard against the pillar, scratched away in a cramped, sweaty scribble, and wanted to throw up.

I had missed a vital piece of information somewhere and would have to ask. I hated to ask. Speaking into an ear in front of me, spacing the question between the buckshot, and feeling like Butch Cassidy talking to the Sundance Kid, I said, ever so quietly, "Who are those guys?" The ear became a face, a pitying face that looked as though it were viewing the decline of democracy in the Western world. "That," he said in a dead tone, "is the leadership."

Oh.

I turned to what I hoped was a more sympathetic ear and asked again.

"I don't know," came the answer in a voice as desperate as my own. "Ask the *New York Times* when it's over."

We write first and ask questions later. It doesn't matter who is talking, just as long as the words get in the notebook. If Allen Funt and the *Candid Camera* crew set themselves up on a street corner in Washington and started talking, eventually every reporter in the city would be there writing furiously and looking around for the *New York Times*.

Standing in the White House driveway one biting January

afternoon, waiting for a group of governors to come out of their meeting with President Reagan, the press crew was like a pack of twitchy greyhounds anticipating the bell and leaping at the mechanical rabbit. Every time the door opened we tightened up, turned on the cameras, and rushed whoever appeared, demanding the words, the words, the words.

"Is that a governor?" shouted one anguished soul in the back, far beyond hearing range. "Are you all talking to a governor up there?"

We were talking to an assistant flunky who had a bunch of press releases, and we tore at his stack of papers like maniacs. When the governors finally did appear to say their piece, they were drowned out by the President's helicopter, which was taking off for the weekend trip to Camp David, and many of us missed a lot of what they had to say. But we got the notes from the reporters up front and stood talking with each other afterward about exactly what was said and what the governors' conference meant.

Press perceptions grow like fungus, and what one paper writes is generally in all papers. During the 1984 presidential election the word went around that "the *Washington Post* is taking Hollings seriously," and we all took another look at Hollings.

When *Time* did a cover story on Nancy Reagan's impact in the Oval Office, the *Washington Post* did a front-page story on the story and noted that "*Time* supports the recurring thesis among Washington's news establishment that Mrs. Reagan is an influential force inside the Reagan White House and sometimes affects policy."

Must be true. It's in all the papers.

Nothing strikes fear in a reporter's heart quite like picking up the *New York Times* and the *Washington Post* in the morning and seeing that the stories in those papers do not match his or her own. Must be wrong. It's in all the other papers. Never mind that a democracy is a million different truths; Washington journalism strives to be a monolith.

We move together in a ritual dance, a kind of "wink-wink, nudge-nudge, we know that they know that we know" minuet with power that has been choreographed in advance and might as well be written in advance. "The White House said . . ." "The State Department reacted . . ." "The Pentagon refused to comment . . ." The buildings talk, the sources are protected, and one begins to have the uneasy feeling that one is writing *for* the power structure, not about it.

Did Ernie Pyle do stakeouts? Would the immortal Hildy Johnson, hero of the play *The Front Page*, have stood around waiting for a bunch of mumblers to come out of a room and say nothing? No, he would have stayed in Chicago with the thugs.

There is something in the atmosphere here that makes one really long for a conversation with a punk, a two-bit gangster, a human being who can explain himself in one or two grubby little phrases with maybe a hand gesture. But instead we get "senior White House officials."

In 1982 after former Israeli Prime Minister Menachem Begin had met with President Reagan, reporters gathered in the White House press room for a briefing with Alexander Haig, who was then secretary of state. White House Deputy Press Secretary Larry Speakes came out first and told us we were to refer to Haig as a "senior White House official." We all dutifully wrote down "senior White House official" and took notes as Haig proceeded to say nothing about the Begin-Reagan meeting except that the President was working to protect "America's vital interests" and that the talks were "frank, extensive, and bordered on blunt."

So, what was the problem with going public with that bit of hash, Al? And more to the point, why didn't all of us heavy hitter reporter types in the room tell the senior White House official either he could be on the record for the folks who paid his salary or he could go pound salt?

Because this is Mount Olympus, that's why. We are the people chosen to climb to the summit and talk to the sun gods. If you talk to a sun god, you've got to show some respect. You don't just bust in there and treat him like the sewer commissioner of Akron. You play the game and do the dance.

When a press aide calls with "a statement from the congressman," we don't tell the readers of the morning paper that the press aide read a statement that the congressman probably never saw and didn't know he made because the aide wrote it.

And we don't tell the readers that many a congressman doesn't know what he's said even after he's said it. At a press conference where Rhode Island Senator Claiborne Pell had spoken in support of a New England historical preservation project, I went up to one of his aides afterward and asked if the senator, who had left for another meeting, would be available later for a phone interview on the project.

"I don't think so," said the aide. "He hasn't been briefed on this yet."

Nobody read that in my story the next day. When it came time to write, I smoothed everything out and played nice. Those are the rules of the game. Just like there is an unwritten law that says congressional hearings are reported as though they are interesting. Rigor mortis may set in as witness after witness reads page after page of boring testimony, but we pick out the flashy sentences and make it sing.

And when some group holds a press conference in a very small room to give the impression that God and everybody showed up to hear its news, we forget to mention that it was trying to fool the television cameras and that three people in a utility closet can look like a multitude.

And when House Speaker Thomas P. O'Neill holds his daily press briefing before the start of the House session, we leave out the part about how reporters regularly bait him to get a juicy quote, and that if left to his own devices, he probably wouldn't say half of what he says on the front pages of the papers. O'Neill, an old-time, low-key Massachusetts pol, is just not a media-mad, snappy-quote kind of guy, but reporters know he'll say something hot if they push the right button. So they keep pushing.

Seeking his reaction to the news that the CIA had circulated a handbook to revolutionaries in Nicaragua in 1984, reporters kept asking over and over for a comment on William Casey's management of the agency. O'Neill was noncommittal, so they asked if he thought Casey was responsible, and wanted to know if he should be fired. Finally, a reporter who sounded as if she were coaching a grade-schooler with his homework said pointedly, "Mr. Speaker, what would you like Mr. Casey to do?"

"I want him to get out of there," the Speaker said, and the reporters ran for the phones to tell their editors that O'Neill had just called for the resignation of Casey.

Most of those "House Speaker Thomas P. O'Neill said yesterday" stories sound as if the guy stood on the Capitol steps with a bullhorn and made a pronouncement, when very often he was just badgered into a corner or thinking out loud, and either way usually looked pretty uncomfortable with the whole process.

I think a lot of us are uncomfortable with the whole process, but figure this is the way things are done, and what do we know, anyway. Coming to Washington is like joining a fraternity, or walking into the high school lunchroom for the first time, or moving to a new cul-de-sac, or any number of terrifying experiences in life where there is a giant THEM and a tiny you. Only the feeling is more so here. I have lived in a lot of cities and cracked into a lot of THEMs, but have yet to feel at home as a reporter in Washington.

Maybe it's because I keep getting Donald Regan mixed up with Ronald Reagan. Maybe it's because a shelf fell on me during my first interview. I was on the phone talking with a man at the State Department when the wall shelf above my desk let go, sending a vase of flowers, a loaded wire in-basket, and a clutch of paper clips onto my lap. The man from the State Department kept talking and I kept writing.

Maybe it's because nobody can pronounce my name. It keeps coming out Susan Trask, Susan Grausch, Suzanne Thrush, Sarah Trusk, Sylvia Traub, or Barbara Fogg. That can get to you, especially Barbara Fogg.

I remember going up to the Hill to get my first press pass. It was a heady moment — being in the U.S. Capitol for the first time; seeing real, live senators in the hall; knowing that the pass would be my ticket to history. I walked up to the man at the desk in the Senate press gallery, and he reached into his files, producing a small white wallet-sized card. I looked down and read it eagerly, and then read it again:

"Susan Trausch, *Toledo Blade*."

I think my biggest problem in Washington is not having any sources. Oh, sure, I've got the press secretaries' numbers — everybody's got those. I'm talking about sources — insiders, oracles, seers, and soothsayers who spill their guts in pay phones or behind the ferns in French restaurants. The people about whom other reporters say cryptically, "Let me check with my sources," and then disappear for two hours or go into the office and shut the door.

If I ever meet someone in a parking garage late at night, it's going to be the attendant with the keys to my car. There is no guarded address book in my purse, and anybody who wants to come in and spin my Rolodex around and look at numbers is welcome, but you'd probably rather visit the National Archives.

I don't have any sources because I never learned how to cultivate them. They're a lot like African violets, and I never had any luck with them, either. I grow geraniums. You can't kill a geranium unless you drive over it with a tank.

Basically, what I like to do is call people up, ask questions, and write stuff down. Dumb questions have never bothered me. Better a dumb question now than a dumb story later. But the typical Washington source expects smart questions, and you don't just call these people up and write stuff down. You court them, invite them out for drinks, play squash with them, "get to know them," visit their camps, and learn their ways.

"Go up to the Hill, hang around, and talk to people," the guys in the bureau told me, but whenever I tried it I felt like a jerk. "Hi there, congressman, I'm hanging around today talking to people who are hanging around, which must mean neither of us has enough to do . . ." I am task-oriented, probably because of early toilet training. I don't "hang around" well. Hanging around always makes me feel like a Christmas wreath left on the house way past Memorial Day.

There was one man on the Hill my *Globe* colleagues said was crucial to reporting life in Washington. He had been a source for everyone in the bureau for years and required quick and deft cultivation by any new recruit. So I quickly and deftly made an appointment to see him. I had often heard the guys talking with this man on the phone and had assumed from all the joviality at our end that he must have been a stand-up comedian before going into politics.

My interview with him sounded like a Quaker meeting. We sat in his office staring at each other for fifteen or twenty minutes while the clock ticked. At one point I asked what seemed like an astute, probing question about "the power of the Massachusetts delegation" and its future with Speaker O'Neill being close to retirement.

The man smiled indulgently, looked at his watch, and said, "You don't really expect me to talk about that, do you?"

That was one of his more detailed answers. So much for deft and quick. It took me nearly three years to figure out that he must have thought this was some kind of trick question to get him to confirm O'Neill's retirement so that I could run to the phone and yell, "Highly placed congressional aide says O'Neill will retire someday." Which is about as interesting as yelling, "O'Neill is in his seventies and has white hair," but these people excite easily.

At least I think that's what he figured. Whatever the problem, this source of sources did not become one of mine, and I came to think of him as "the sphinx."

"He won't talk unless you ask the right questions," I was told. "You've got to let him know that you know what's going on."

So, if I knew what was going on, why would I need to talk to him?

To confirm the prevailing opinion, that's why. The reason people talk to each other is to hear what they think they already know. Since nothing is really happening, sources are needed to bolster theories more than they are needed to provide facts. My approach to reporting had always been to start at square one and work through until the picture becomes clear. In Washington that's like trying to be a surveyor in a quicksand pit.

To make conversation flow more easily I was told to use nicknames whenever possible, slap people on the back, and say with feeling, "Hey, Jimmy, how the hell are ya!" I did this about as well as I hung around. I tried it once with a press secretary named William whom I had never met. I dialed his office, leaned back in the desk chair, and cavalierly asked for "Billy."

"Billy who?" the receptionist asked stiffly. "There's no Billy in our office."

"Er, William, the press secretary," I said, rolling back up into hunch position over the phone.

"Oh," she said. "You mean Pete."

"Pete?" I asked. "William is Pete?"

"He's been Pete all his life," she said.

It's hard to be cool when you're out of it, and I always seemed to be two or three events behind.

In 1982 I was assigned to fill in for the *Globe*'s regular White House reporter and cover one of Ronald Reagan's congressional campaign swings to Illinois and Nebraska. I'd never traveled with a President before and wanted to do it right. On the morning of the trip I woke up early and studied my wardrobe, deciding on the conservative yet chic "dress for success" brown suit and matching pumps. I did my nails, took extra time with the hair, and worked to get the eyeliner straight. Then I called a taxi and headed for Andrews Air Force Base.

"On the road with the President today?" the cabbie asked, smiling, and I figured I must look the part. I had a light coat and one small overnight case on the seat beside me, and gave myself points for looking uncluttered and efficient.

"Do you work with Lesley Stahl?" the driver wanted to know. I upped his tip a couple of bucks.

But walking into the check-in area at Andrews, I felt the cold fingers of fear closing around the ruffled collar of my high-necked blouse. Most everybody in the room was wearing down parkas, slacks, and boots. Either these people knew something or I'd mistakenly hooked up with a charter flight to the Yukon. As I sat down to watch my suit wrinkle, I heard a cameraman nearby bellow to a co-worker: "They say we'll be up to our ankles in shit at a pig farm."

We were, and the brown pumps died in it.

No doubt there had been some kind of briefing somewhere before this trip but I had missed it. That was the story of my life in Washington. No matter how organized I tried to be, I missed the briefing and usually wound up stepping in something.

After the defeat of the Equal Rights Amendment in 1982, I covered a press conference given by former Democratic Massachusetts Senator Paul Tsongas and representatives of women's groups who had gathered to announce that the senator had reintroduced the legislation. They talked about the historic moment of beginning again and acted as though this were the first congressional move being made to revive the amendment after its defeat.

But two weeks earlier Representative Mario Biaggi of New York had reintroduced the bill in the House, which seemed significant — to my mind, at any rate — and sounded like one of those briefing facts that should not be missed. So, I raised my hand and said, "Didn't Mario Biaggi already do this?" People looked at me with that squint usually reserved for weirdos on the street. Whether Biaggi or ten other people already filed it in the House wasn't the point. This was the Senate and everybody was making speeches and this was news.

I had never related well to news and had come to Washington to write feature stories. That was another problem. They frown on that here. Feature writing is the Rodney Dangerfield of Washington journalism. You don't get no respect unless you've got a hot one from or for the corridors of power. Call the White House asking to talk with people about how the President makes up his Christmas card list and how he gets them all addressed, and the yawn is audible.

"There was a press advisory mailed out on that last week," they say.

Tell them you don't want a press advisory, you want to talk to real breathing human beings on the card committee sitting at a table addressing envelopes, and they don't see why this is at all interesting.

Tell congressional aides that you want to do a story on the archaic language of Congress and why legislators have to say "the gentleman from New Jersey" instead of "Mr. Jones," which would be a heck of a lot less confusing for everybody, and the congressional aides are curt. They're too busy preparing a statement for their boss to read on the floor to tell you why he has to talk funny when he gets there.

People in government jobs are given special training in turning off feature writers. They are taught to say things like, "That story has been done by every paper in the country twice," or "Why are you looking at that?" or "Call me next spring if I'm not out of the country."

Which is why the folks who write regularly for the *New York Times* Washington Talk page should get some kind of medal. This is the section with the light stuff: humor and off-the-wall gossip that saves the paper from terminal objectivity. I know they do not lead easy lives, these people who go forth to bring the history of Senate Bean Soup or the peace of Dumbarton Oaks to the inside pages while their studious, straight-faced colleagues are hard at it with the White House policy shift on page one. But they continue to continue, and I salute them.

Feature writers in Washington are like members of a resistance movement. They speak quietly in corners, pass around funny news releases, exchange clippings, and tell each other to hang tough with whimsy and that it's okay to go to stakeouts and find the Ohio Clock more interesting than the senators.

The Ohio Clock, a massive grandfather number outside room 211 on the Senate side of the Capitol, is a primary stakeout landmark on the Hill. Notices are posted telling reporters to meet at the appointed hour "under the Ohio Clock," and it has become part of the lexicon as a kind of spreading chestnut tree for major events. But turn to a colleague waiting for a door to open and ask how he thinks the antique got its name, and he will say, absently, "I never really thought about it," meaning, "I don't want to think about that because it's not important." He won't care that it was built the year Ohio became a state or that, contrary to logical assumption, its works came from Philadelphia. This is certainly not a fact that needs to be committed to memory, but it should be at least remotely interesting to a supposedly naturally curious reporter who has to spend a lot of time standing under the thing.

But Washington reporters tend to be curious about what those in power and other reporters have determined is the major news of the day. There's really not much room for anything else. I think that may explain why hundreds of reporters worked in the chaos of the National Press Building during three years of remodeling and never wrote about it. The bricks crashing through ceilings, the exposed wiring, the doors opening onto six-foot drops, and the rats and bulldozers running up and down the halls were not considered news by very many people.

"If this were going on at the White House or a government building in town, you'd see it on *Sixty Minutes*," said one bureau chief in the building.

But it was happening right over their heads so they missed it. They were too busy watching slides under the microscope to notice the roof coming down, too self-absorbed to see what was happening to themselves.

I think it's time for everybody here to start looking around a little more. We need to ditch this notion that we who type and the people we cover in Washington are special, that this is the pinnacle of careers, journalistic and political, and that we have all arrived to flex our muscles for each other. Yes, the press is a vital part of democracy, but the cozier we get with power the less vital we become. A whole pecking order and star status has developed in the press, just as there is in the hierarchy we cover. There are "those who know," those who are "close to Baker," or who "have dinner with Dole." What we've built here in this supposed citadel of free access is one of the most exclusionary shops in the world.

In short, we're being used most of the time, loving it, and writing a lot of glop. The national press corps could easily be turning into the national press corpse. All it'll take is one more letter and a couple more stakeouts.

9

Somebody
Pull the Plug

THE SOUND OF wire-service machines is permanently recorded in my mind's ear as the identifying noise of Washington. Incessant, demanding, self-important, it will ever be the pulse of the nation's capital.

When I am sitting on the porch of the rest home, rocking back and forth in my twilight, someone will say "Washington," and I will instantly hear the *clack, clack, clack, ding-ding* of the two machines that sat in the hallway of the *Boston Globe* bureau, never shutting up no matter what, taunting me with the endless lists of events, the tight little capsules of what was happening where I wasn't and wouldn't get to in time because it drove me crazy deciding where to go.

Come to think of it, maybe nobody will have to say "Washington" at all on the porch of the home. Maybe the sound will stay in my head forever. Maybe I will just sit there in a corner going *clack, clack, clack, ding-ding* to myself all day. And people will shake their heads and say, "What's with that one?" And someone will answer quietly, "Wire machines, Washington, terrible thing. She couldn't keep up."

They were relentless, those two machines, Associated Press and United Press International, the Siamese twins of journalism, spewing out mountains of identical copy into the night, overnight, through the weekend, at the crack of dawn. It was the first noise I'd hear coming down the hall to the bureau. The machines dominated the reception area, demanded attention immediately, rode over conversations, and cut into thoughts. When nobody was around, I kicked them occasionally or slapped their little sides silly and told them to knock it off, but they only seemed to clack louder.

Back at the *Globe* city room in Boston and at other newspapers, I had thought of the wire machine as my friend, a sunny little creature that chattered pleasantly in corners and waited patiently for its paper to be ripped. In Washington they were like those fiendish marching brooms in Walt Disney's version of *The Sorcerer's Apprentice*, furiously bringing in bucket after bucket of water long after the workroom had flooded. They knew their power. They knew that not to follow the wires, not to know what was going on all over the city every single minute, was to twist slowly, slowly in the wind.

I worked with people who ripped and read, ripped and read, folded wire copy into their pockets, raced with it flying out behind them back to their desks, made calls, made lists, and held the picture of the day and its news in their heads the way an air traffic controller knows the flight patterns on the screen. Every time I went out there and read I got confused and tense. Sometimes I ripped, sometimes I didn't. Sometimes days would go by and I wouldn't read or rip. What was news? What was truth? As a feature writer I didn't have a specific beat and was more or less turned loose to write "off the news" stuff or human interest pieces or whatever was happening. And so, theoretically, I had to pay attention to nothing in particular but everything in general, which meant decisions, news sense, judgment, and savvy.

"You're missing something, missing something, missing something . . ." the clacking seemed to be saying, and I would go back and rip, saving piles of wire copy in a basket that would get sorted and resorted, the way the guy with the grapefruits must have sorted.

If you've never heard of the guy with the grapefruits, that's an old joke from Sid Caesar's show or maybe it was the *Jackie Gleason Show* or the *Ernie Kovacs Show*. But it has lived in my family for years, and all somebody has to say is, "I feel like the guy with the grapefruits," and everybody at the table laughs. I forget the punch line, but the point was that the guy with the grapefruits had to sort them and put them in boxes: big ones in one box, little ones in another box, medium-size ones in yet another. An impossible task when one is faced with a ton of grapefruits because one must sit there and continually compare and contrast, asking philosophical questions like, "Is this really big, or does it just look big now because it happens to be rolling around the floor with a bunch of smaller ones?"

And so I would sit there sorting the big stories from the mediums and smalls, listening to the wire machine clacking out more, and getting hives on my neck. That's what happens when I get uptight. Two hives under the right ear lobe. And don't ask if they're small, medium, or large.

A Washington correspondent is on the front lines, a stranger in a strange land, E.T. phoning home with word from Uncle Sam. But the question is, What word do you phone home with? There are so many of them from so many different directions.

Clack, clack, clack, ding-ding . . . This just in . . . Undersecretary of state for economic affairs to address conference titled "Retrospective on the Bonn Summit."

I think hard about the Bonn summit. When was it? What was it? Where was it? Why do we need to look back at it? Should I go and find out? Could this eventually lead to a story on summits and how they grew? Does anybody in Boston care about summits and how they grew? Should I call and find out or use my head?

Clack, clack, clack . . . Foreign Policy Association and the

World Affairs Council sponsoring panel discussion titled "Great Decisions and the World in 1985."

Awesome. I should definitely call Boston. Then again, maybe I should go and then call Boston. Better yet, maybe I should wait until 1986 and see if they knew what they were talking about and say nothing to Boston. Why can't I think of one decision that would affect the world in 1985? Why can't I think of any that affected the world in 1975? The hives are killing me.

Clack, clack . . . Former Secretary of State Alexander Haig will address the National Press Club on "Europe and the World."

Maybe he's planning to take over both. Better go.

Clack, clack, clack . . . *Washington Post* columnist Haynes Johnson to discuss "What America Is Thinking" at U.S. Chamber of Commerce Association Insiders Meeting.

Could be he knows what Boston is thinking, and if I talk to him, I won't have to call home. Amazing how one man can know what America is thinking, but then, he *does* work for the *Washington Post.* Amazing also that a bunch of hotshot insiders don't already know what America is thinking. What are they doing in there, and why don't they get out more and sort grapefruits?

Clack, ding, clack, ding-ding . . . "Advisory." The machine has an advisory. Stop the presses. What is an advisory? At 2 P.M. the Pentagon will hold "an embargoed advance background press briefing" on Soviet military power. Should I go just to see what an embargoed advance background briefing is? Would that be a waste of time? Do I care if it is? I need an advisory advisory.

Clack, ding, clack, ding-ding . . . Yet another advisory from the Pentagon. This time they are holding "an on-the-record, single-subject briefing" on the establishment of a new officer program "to enhance efficiency and management effectiveness in the navy." There's more. The advisory advises that "the briefing will be conducted under a 'vespers' format, meaning no cameras will be permitted and tape recorders may be used only for note-taking purposes."

I feel a numbness on the right side of the head.

Clack, clack . . . Economist William Cox of the Congressional Research Service to address the National Economists Club on "Can the World Live with Floating Exchange Rates?"

The antennae go up. I didn't spend nine years as a Business page reporter for nothing. Exchange rates are very big, especially when they float. They are also very dull. They are big, floating, and dull, like a giant bar of Ivory soap. The antennae go down. Actually, one goes up and one stays down and the hives get bigger.

Clack, clack, clack . . . Institute for Policy Studies holds seminar on "The Labor Upsurge in Brazil." Could be important. Upsurges usually are. So are downsurges. Anything that surges has an urgency about it that puts it in the upper third of the basket.

Clackity clack, clackity clack . . . Press briefing at the American Petroleum Institute on the subject "Coping with Lead Phasedown."

I don't want to cope with lead phasedown. I don't even want to know what it is. But I save it in case Boston does.

Clack, clackity ding . . . A day-long conference titled "Reassessing the Political Spectrum," sponsored by the Cato Institute.

I see the word "Cato" and think of Peter Sellers as Inspector Clouseau with his manservant, the karate expert. I see the scene where Clouseau walks into the silent, dark apartment waiting for the inevitable leap from Cato — or maybe it was Kato — who at one point was on top of the canopy bed. I think about Peter Sellers movies for a good twenty minutes and lose track of the political spectrum. What color is the political spectrum, anyway? And if a person hasn't even assessed it a first time, would it do any good to write about reassessing it? Bottom of the pile. "Small" box.

Clack, clack, clackity clackity . . . The Federal Communications Commission is meeting to consider whether AM radio stations that are allowed to operate only during the daytime should get special consideration if they apply for new FM licenses just becoming available.

There are radio stations in Boston. Mid-pile. "Medium" box.

Clack, clack, clack . . . Transportation Table lunch on the topic "Is There a Future for High-speed Rail?"

They have trains in Boston.

Ding, clack, ding . . . Federal Library and Information Center Committee sponsors workshop on "Measuring Productivity in Libraries."

They have a library in Boston, but it's not productive. How can a library be productive? A productive library would be like a productive art museum. Nobody would go in there if it was productive. The whole point of libraries and museums is to waste time.

Clackity clackity, ding, clack . . . A man from Lucedale, Mississippi, will be in the Capital Centre in Landover, Maryland, this morning to demonstrate his nine-thousand-pound energy machine, which "produces greater external energy output than external energy input."

Energy is big in Boston. People talk about it constantly. They had an energy crisis up there in the seventies. But the guy sounds like a nut, especially since he's giving out quotes about a court case he's involved in. Then again, maybe he has invented something that could replace Congress. Probably worth a look . . . if there wasn't all this other stuff, if the phone wasn't ringing, if the hives weren't itching.

Clack, clack, clack . . . Press preview of Smithsonian exhibition "Mammals in the Limelight."

I am a mammal; I should go. I see the lead character in the play *Skin of Our Teeth* beginning his talk to the convention of the world with the words "Fellow mammals . . ." I am off to Peter Sellers country again. Nothing sorted for a half hour.

Ding-ding-ding . . . Treasury Secretary James Baker will

hold a press conference on tax reform at the Treasury Department in the cash room.

I want to see the cash room really badly. I wonder if there is a cash bar in the cash room. I wonder if there is cash in the cash room. Must be. This is a very literal bunch. Nobody would call it the cash room to be flip. Make note to call Treasury and ask about cash room so I don't have to sit through press conference on tax reform. Top of the pile.

Clack, clackity, ding . . . The National Institutes of Health opens three-day Consensus Conference on Travelers' Diarrhea.

And I thought hives were bad. Three days of diarrhea. Presumably, the consensus will be that it exists. No Montezuma jokes, though.

Ding, ding, ding . . . Another list coming over: "Top Stories in Sight at This Hour." We have David Stockman saying the budget "has problems in many places." Organized labor is mad at the White House, the White House wants to get Amtrak, a U.S. weather satellite has died, and there's trouble in Peru.

Every hour the sightings change, the focus shifts. What's important now was not important then and won't be important this afternoon.

Clack, clackity clack . . . Students for America, a street theater group, dressed as Sandinista troopers, will abduct members of Congress and their staffs and carry them to symbolic concentration camp on the west front lawn of the Capitol.

Clack, ding, clack . . . Senator Russell Long is keynote speaker at seminar of the American Gas Association.

Clack, clack, clack . . . National Space Club reception for members of Congress.

Clackity clack, clack . . . Department of Energy secretary to dedicate bicycle rack.

Clack, clack, clackity, ding . . . Slicing and eating of the largest submarine sandwich ever assembled — an estimated six hundred feet long.

Ding, clackity, ding . . . Southwest Jazz Ballet Company of Houston will salute the Pentagon on Flag Day with a performance marking the first ever by a dance company at ground zero.

Clack, clack, clack . . . Meeting of the Schizophrenia Association of Greater Washington.

Clackity clack, clackity clack . . . Cake cutting at Fort McNair to mark 210th anniversary of the U.S. Army.

Ding-ding, clack, clack clack . . . Institute for Policy Studies holding seminar titled "Madness and Politics: A Study of Mental Illness and Political Events."

Somebody else has been saving the wires.

10

Smithfield DeWitt
Is Picking His Nose . . .

THE EXPERTS TELL ME that the goal of a feature writer in the nation's capital should be to write profiles of famous people.

"That's what you want to do," they say, and they should know because they have been here for years and have learned to read them without cracking up.

I am working on it. Every day I read a *Washington Post* Style page profile and come closer to writing in italics and thinking only in the present tense. Every month I read *Washingtonian* magazine, particularly the People to Watch section, as well as analyzing *Dossier* and *Diplomatic Dossier* magazines for variations on the genre. After several years of study I think I'm beginning to nail this thing down, and offer here a sample of the profile prose that has helped make Washington what it is today — a place where reader, writer, and subject can all feel important when they go to the newsstand in the morning.

Naturally, I wanted to find the ultimate famous person for the interview and by sheer coincidence was able to hook up with the incomparable Smithfield DeWitt — author, actor, producer, tennis pro, White House aide, attorney, candidate for the Senate, candidate for the House, candidate for President, gourmet cook, bon vivant, and spy.

I met him on the subway.

There he was, sitting in a corner seat writing a novel, memorizing lines to a play, practicing his serve, speaking into a microphone in his breast pocket, studying a speech, waving to fellow passengers, smiling rakishly to himself, and eating truffles. That seemed to be a lot of activity even for a rush hour ride on the D.C. Metro, so I walked over and asked him if he was a famous person who had been profiled yet by the Washington press corps.

He said he was so famous he couldn't stand himself, but somehow the media hadn't gotten around to him yet.

"There's a famous-person glut, you know," he explained. "They can't get to us all, and by the time they do some of us won't be famous anymore. It's very sad."

I promised to do my best to put him on the journalistic map, set up an interview for the following week, and wrote the following story:

NEW YORK — Smithfield DeWitt is waiting.

The plane is an hour late, the traffic is backed up coming from the airport and *THE* Smithfield DeWitt is *WAITING*. *Omigod!*

One doesn't keep Smithfield DeWitt waiting, even if one is a well-known Washington journalist who interviews heavy hitters all the time, appears regularly on talk shows, and has a couple of book contracts in the fire.

The cab creeps through the Manhattan traffic, the adrenaline pumps through the veins, and the reporter finally arrives, breathless, at the hotel room of His Greatness.

An assistant opens the door and motions the visitor into a plush suite, tastefully appointed in oriental carpeting, art deco lamps, and Naugahyde chairs. And there, amid a pile of listening devices, word processors, books, tennis balls, and

125

Cuisinarts stands the man of a thousand careers, the ubiquitous Smithfield DeWitt.

There is a tense pause before he softens slightly and remembers that he has chosen this reporter from among all others to do the first-ever exclusive one-on-one interview with him in his world-renowned suite at the Plaza — eat your heart out, *People* magazine.

Smithfield DeWitt, a distinguished fifty-two, graying at the temples, extends a large, firm hand in welcome and invites the visitor to sit down. But he himself does not sit down. He chooses instead to pace back and forth with wires dangling, papers rustling, tennis racket fanning the air, and truffle crumbs dropping on the rug.

He seems restless, this big, tall, towering inferno of a man who walks with a kind of intense but thoughtful swagger, sorting out what he wants to say and what he doesn't want to say, how he wants to say it and how he doesn't want to say it. He is in full pace now, striding the length of the room, hunching his shoulders forward, frowning at the truffle crumbs, and picking his nose.

Yes, Smithfield DeWitt is picking his nose. *PICKING HIS NOSE!* It is not easy to do with everything he is holding in his hands, but he manages, and in so doing reveals that essence of self, that inner core of his very being that has catapulted him to where he is. For it is just this kind of bold, warts-and-all human gesture that has given his writing, acting, tennis, candidacies, espionage, White House advising, lawsuits, parties, and cooking the sense of realism that has become his trademark.

Shoulders still hunched, forefinger aloft, Smithfield DeWitt looks directly at his visitor and says, "So you want to ask me some questions here, or what?"

It is a challenge, an invitation to intellectual combat, but the visitor is ready. Smithfield DeWitt is bluntly and with an equally direct gaze asked exactly why he keeps this world-renowned suite at the Plaza when he has a world-renowned town house in Georgetown and does most of his work in

Washington. And furthermore, why is it that reporter and subject are not talking to each other in Washington, where they both live?

"Ah!" he says pointedly. "Because we are who we are — Washington interviewer and interviewee, both of whom look more exciting when they travel. You get on a plane, I get on a plane, and everybody's impressed that we are so busy and going so many places to talk with so many influential people, no?"

It is obvious how Smithfield DeWitt got to the top of his professions. The power is unmistakable; the chutzpah, tangible. This is most assuredly the creator of the novels *Politics and the Brooklyn Bridge* and *Bootsie Goes to the Pentagon*. This is the prosecuting attorney in the famed Frickheimer whiplash case, the man who whispers in the ears of presidents, campaigns for everything that has an election, cooks in lead pots, and has plainly *Been There*, seen, remembered, and written down.

"I've *Been There*, seen, remembered, and written down," he is saying. "That's the kind of guy I am. That's why you're interviewing me, sucking every bit of alleged humanity you can out of me, putting it into a hundred or so bitchy yet fawning lines and confirming the fact that we are both indispensable to the republic."

The man is *Awesome*.

"And don't forget to write it in the present tense," he adds. "That way you give it a sense of immediacy and intimacy. You freeze-dry me in time in a Ziploc bag of prose, forever pacing, forever picking my nose, creating the illusion that you are writing about a full, complete human being."

Smithfield DeWitt is sitting now and leaning forward in the big brown Naugahyde chair. Subjects of profile interviews either lean back or lean forward in big chairs, and Smithfield DeWitt is decidedly a forward leaner. The tension has not left his body, and he seems to be mentally pacing. He lights up a cigarette, watches the smoke curl over his head, and asks quickly, "Did you notice the brand? Carlton 100's menthol.

You put the brand a person smokes in a profile, and people think you're really hot stuff in the observation department."

Smithfield DeWitt is puffing his Carlton 100's menthols and talking about his decision to follow a dozen career paths at once.

"It just sort of happened," he is saying, looking out the window. The sun is glinting off his rimless glasses, and his face viewed from the side exposes his Dick Tracy jutting jaw.

"Dad wanted me to work the farm, but I figured, if I was going to be shoveling cow manure for a living, why not go to Washington? I got my law degree and then the doors just started opening. The White House called, the CIA called, Hollywood called, television called, the book publishers called, you found me on the subway, and the rest is history."

He pauses, snuffs out his Carlton 100 menthol in the ashtray, and then adds, "Another factor you have to take into consideration is that I'm as crazy as a bedbug."

The rakish smile plays about his lips again. Smithfield DeWitt watches it for a while and then says quietly, "Not many other places for a rakish smile to play anymore, are there?"

The devastating DeWitt wit at its best. Not for nothing has the man become known as "the master of the unsettling phrase." His parties, of course, are legend — the water balloon fights, the trick birthday candles, the strategically placed plastic vomit, the rubber spiders, and the ice cube down the back.

It seems incredible that no one has snapped him up for a profile before, and he is asked to elaborate on his theory that there is a "famous-person glut" in the nation's capital.

"Not just in Washington," he says, the facial muscles tightening, the body springing into pace position once again. "It's everywhere. All over America. All over the world."

Smithfield DeWitt is angry now, too angry to pick his nose, even, as he begins to talk about the canker that is gnawing at his multiprofessional soul.

"We've got famous people up the wazoo," he is saying, fairly spitting the words across the room. "There are more famous people than there are obscure people today. In fact it's getting so bad that obscure people are almost becoming better reading than famous ones. This gets to me. Sometimes late at night I wake up in a cold sweat thinking that your basic average Joe in Toledo is more exciting than I am!"

What's this? The great Smithfield DeWitt *unsure* of himself? It hardly seems possible. But listen to him talk:

"I'm unsure of myself — do you hear me? — *unsure!*" he is saying. "It hardly seems possible. But listen to me talk. Okay, I can write, act, produce, cook, spy, advise, defend, prosecute, lob, run for office, and be scintillating twenty-four hours a day, but is that enough? What good is it if I don't get profiled regularly and people aren't told that I'm as famous as they think I am? What good is it if every associate undersecretary, every two-bit congressman with a pretty face, every flash-in-the-pan trendy writer gets a profile too?"

Smithfield DeWitt is walking to the door. He is opening it.

"It's all your fault," he is saying. "You write this superficial crapola — nothing great like *Bootsie Goes to the Pentagon* or anything — and people like me start becoming dependent on you. I want you out of my world-renowned Plaza suite right now, and if I see you on my plane back to Washington, I'm opening a window. Don't ever bother me on the subway again, either."

Smithfield DeWitt is coming apart at the seams and the interview appears to be ending. This is probably not a good time to bring up the beating *Bootsie Goes to the Pentagon* is taking from the literary critics, but what the hell.

Smithfield DeWitt is grabbing the visitor by the throat and the assistant is brandishing a cattle prod. Timing is everything.

Chased down twelve flights of steps, the visitor races the cattle prod to a cab, heads for the airport, flings the notebook into the East River, and books a nonstop flight to Toledo to interview this Joe person.

11

Hello, Good-bye

I'm late, I'm late
For a very important date.
No time to say hello, goodbye —
I'm late, I'm late, I'm late.
    — the White Rabbit,
    Alice's Adventures
    in Wonderland

IT'S BEEN SAID that people in Washington really don't know whether they're coming or going. This is understandable, considering how much time they spend running for things — planes, trains, buses, subways, taxis, and, of course, their seats.

The average government official is either just getting into town, just leaving, or up in the air somewhere over Greenland. People who aren't arriving or leaving are meeting somebody who is, or are on their way to or from an airport, train station, or bus depot in a fast car. And if they're not arriving, departing, en route, meeting somebody, or riding in a fast car, then they're giving a briefing on where they've been or being briefed on where they are about to go. And the chances are pretty good that the briefing will be across town, requiring at least a taxi ride or, at best, a police escort and a motorcade.

This isn't a city — it's a terminal, a perpetual motion machine of entrances and exits. The congressional delegation comes in from a two-week work period in the home district and immediately heads out for a fact-finding mission to

Buenos Aires. The President returns from his ten-day economic summit, hits a photo session in the East Room with dignitaries from Tunisia, and then takes the helicopter to Camp David. The dignitaries from Tunisia spend the next two days riding back and forth between the embassy and the State Department in a black limousine with a flag on the hood before heading back to the airport, where they pass the congressional delegation getting in from Buenos Aires. The congressional delegation goes to the State Department for a briefing, holds a news conference on the Hill, and then runs to catch a plane back to the home district as a busload of constituents is being herded through the office for a quick handshake.

The slogan for the District of Columbia is "Washington — a Capital City," but somehow I've never felt that quite captures the mood. "Nice to See You — Gotta Run" would seem to be a lot more appropriate. And it would look great printed on T-shirts, mugs, and license plates over the figure of a person running backward and waving.

Life is lived in fragments here. People pop in and out of rooms clutching lists that have every time slot filled deep into the night. The lists are usually printed on pocket-size index cards for easy minute-by-minute referral during entrances and exits. I know a woman who has pared the index card down to code letters that she prints minutely in ink on her hand, because pulling the card out of her pocket again and again is too time consuming. If she washes her hands, she's dead.

"The congressman is running a little late," the aides always say, looking at their watches, checking the calendar, and offering visitors newspapers, magazines, and coffee. Going to see members of Congress is a bit like going to the doctor — they're overbooked, they can't really do too much about your headache, and they cost a lot.

When they do finally arrive, they're usually concentrating so hard on where they've been and where they're going that it's very difficult for them to deal with where they are. That's why they look that way — frozen smile, tight shoulders, and dilated pupils. What's happened is that they've gone blank. Either they can't remember what their chief aides have told them about who is in the room and why, or they've just remembered that they will be up in the air somewhere over Greenland that night without any clean underwear.

In such a state it's almost impossible to interact with another human being. Not that Washington ever relates well to human beings even under the best of circumstances. Washington understands people only in particular contexts. They are seen in terms of the public works hearing or the anti-nuclear petition or the fund-raising committee. Met as individuals in the middle of the street with no agenda, they mean nothing.

Close friendships are a rarity here. Expedient friendships are formed and easily broken. People are bluntly pragmatic about using each other: having dinner with a source to get information or with a reporter to plant a leak; getting to know a committee chairman because he has access to a senator; and writing a "Dear Chip" letter to someone they barely know and haven't spoken to for years but need to hit for a campaign contribution.

I have lived in five cities and made friends easily in all of them except Washington. There is a wall between people and an explicit message that says from the word go: friendship is not the point. Exactly what the point is I haven't quite figured out, but the warm, casual, easy-welcome threads that connect so nicely between people in other cities simply do not grow here.

New in town, I tried to get to know a woman who worked for another paper. She was the friend of a friend, and I figured we'd have a lot in common, and she would happily show me the ropes in the big city. After trying to make several appointments with her for dinner or drinks, I figured out from the silences and excuses that she wasn't interested in chitchat for chitchat's sake. She made her meals count. She sent out invitations with RSVP on them and had networking brunches.

I think networking is about as much fun as pounding rocks together. The idea is that one is supposed to "make contacts" over the quiche pan, put the contact's name in the Rolodex, and then whip it out at the appropriate moment and say, "We met at the networking brunch and I need to exploit you now." This is considered flattering to the people being called and, in fact, they tend to feel left out if a couple of weeks have gone by during which nobody has tried to exploit them.

When someone says, "You really ought to get to know people in town," they don't mean fun times at the Trivial Pursuit board. They mean joining the Capitol Hill squash club, or breaking grapefruit with White House aides at the Thursday breakfast group. You don't just call someone up in Washington and say, "How the hell are you? Let's get a pizza and shoot the bull." You call with a purpose, get to the point, and make it fast.

A year passed in the *Boston Globe* Washington Bureau before anyone I worked with suggested going out for lunch. This was not part of some evil plot to make me miserable — this was simply Washington. It was the other side of the world from the *Globe*'s office up in Boston, which, like that city, is very familial. Here reporters don't want to know about each other's lives and rarely comment on a story a colleague has in the paper. They are loners, separate entities, each traveling by his or her own power packs.

And I am guilty of it. My social skills have warped. I have a list of people that I keep meaning to call but don't. In Boston I would have called them. In Washington a kind of paralysis set in. Surrounded by this grand sweep of events and sucked into so many parts of it during the week, I hit the off-hours with a strong impulse to fold. I found my sense of reality shifting, too, after a year or so. Instead of being shocked at the lack of communication between people, I was amazed whenever people opened their mouths and actually said something.

I remember having my mind more or less blown when a television reporter told me she was depressed. These people aren't allowed to get depressed. It's in their contracts. They wear red, suck in their cheeks, and look confident twenty-four hours a day. This woman and I barely knew each other, but as we walked back to the Capitol after covering a story in a Senate office building, she said quietly that she felt as though the bottom had dropped out of her life. I wanted to blow a whistle so that everything would stop, sit down on a bench, and discuss this for the rest of the afternoon. But the conversation lasted only a few minutes. She had just had a painful breakup with a man and was questioning whether life in Washington was worth it. Since she opened up, I did also and said I'd been questioning life in Washington since driving into the place.

"I'll tell you what motivates people here," she said. "Fear. They're afraid they're going to fail. You're scared, I'm scared, so we don't talk to each other."

That conversation took place several years ago, and we haven't talked since.

Scared people keep moving. That's the first rule of politics and its environs: keep moving. Moving people look busy, and if they look busy, the public will think they're doing something. Also, they'll be less likely to get hit with a tomato. The second rule seems to be: always try to move in a direction away from your capital, and the farther the better. I think the people who run the world decided relatively early on in history that nothing could be accomplished in Washington or any other capital and that the only sensible course of action was to go somewhere else and talk about accomplishing things. That's why Margaret Thatcher likes to come here and Ronald Reagan likes to go there. In those pictures you see of them smiling and exchanging witticisms, one is usually saying to the other, "Better your capital than mine, sweetheart."

Politicians on the road have a stature and credibility that is almost impossible to achieve when they are surrounded by their government. When President Jaafar Nimeiri came here from Sudan in 1985, for instance, he was hosted, toasted, treated to terrific lunches, and driven around in a fancy car with a chauffeur. When he got back home, his administration had been overthrown in a coup. Obviously, the guy would have had a lousy time if he'd tried to entertain in the palace.

Traveling heads of state give their staff and press corps a real lift. Even though they may say what they've been saying at home for years, it takes on new significance if they say it on top of the Great Wall. And if the pronouncement comes at a summit conference, they sound positively cosmic. That's why they have summit meetings. The very name "summit" suggests a gathering of sages on the mountaintop. Actually, not much is happening up there at all. People go in and out of rooms, in and out of cars, to and away from tables, raise and lower wine glasses, and then stand in a long line to wave for the seven o'clock news while whispering "Better your capital than mine" to whoever drew the short straw at the last summit meeting.

An added benefit of having the summit conference away from home is that the leader can return and proclaim the visit a success. This is not easy to do if it's been all over his capital for a week and people are really sick of the show. Holding one's arms in the air and shouting "It's great to be back" looks pretty ridiculous in the home town, and the conquering-hero image doesn't quite come off.

Whenever the lesser political lights in Congress or the diplomatic ranks hit the road, they try to emulate these summit gatherings and return in the hopes of looking presidential. They try as hard as they can to meet with people who are close to the top, and if they can't get to the top, they make up for it by covering a lot of countries in a short time. In March 1985 Vice President George Bush traveled 28,164 miles in two weeks, and the *Post* announced: "Globe-Spanning Mission Strengthens Bush for '88." The paper described him as going "from the sandstorms of sub-Saharan Africa to the chill of Moscow and then to the heat of Grenada, Honduras and Brazil."

Most of Washington would kill for press like that. There is a certain look politicians get when they talk to reporters about an impending trip — a combination of relief and hope that borders on the inspirational. "This is it," they seem to be saying, "the big one." They stand tall, the chin lifts, and they exude a sense of adventure. They are going "out there," much as Margaret Mead went to Samoa. They will see real Americans in their natural habitat, or real Europeans or real Nicaraguans. And if they travel fast enough and far enough, maybe they'll be able to gain some perspective about what's on their desks. Better yet, they might not have to deal with it at all. I've always had the feeling that's why Utah Senator Jake Garn went up in the space shuttle.

In September 1985 members of the House Ways and Means Committee announced that they were going to a resort in the Virginia hills for a weekend so that they could "think" and "get something done." Gives you a good idea what life is like for them in town.

There is almost no place a congressman won't go. I'm not saying they haven't found facts on those fact-finding missions, but when they go to the Virgin Islands to investigate slow mail service between the islands and the states, you wonder. That trip was noted in a 1983 study on congressional travel done by the public interest group Congress Watch, which says that inadequate reporting procedures and difficulty of public access to the records give elected officials virtual carte blanche on travel. The Congress Watch report included word of a trip by Representative Glenn English, who led a six-member delegation to Nassau, in the Bahamas, and Key West and Miami to "hold hearings and conduct inspections on the subject of drug interdiction and implementation of posse comitatus," whatever that means.

Here are a few other junkets included in the study:

Senator Alfonse D'Amato, along with his father and an

administrative assistant, visited Rome, Naples, "and other places as necessary" in Italy to deliver a check for disaster relief.

Representative Joseph Addabbo took three other representatives, their spouses, five staffers, and four military escorts to Hong Kong, New Zealand, and Samoa "to travel to the Western and Southern Pacific areas to review mutual defense programs in that part of the world."

Senator Barry Goldwater and Senator John Tower both led separate delegations to the Farnborough Air Show in London. Goldwater's trip cost $124,121, and Tower's cost $62,755.

Some travel is necessary, but I'd be willing to bet most of it isn't. When House Speaker Tip O'Neill took twelve Democratic and Republican House members to the Soviet Union to meet the new Soviet leader, Mikhail Gorbachev, in 1985, and then stopped in Spain on the way back, I doubt that great insights were gained on either side, especially considering O'Neill's comment when he landed at Andrews Air Force Base. "The fellow is provocative," O'Neill said of Gorbachev, "but with a sense of charm about him. . . . Do I see a breakthrough in policy? I can't say I see a breakthrough in policy."

For this they could have stayed home, or gone across town to the Russian embassy and sat on the lawn.

Generally, what happens when politicians go on safari is that they take Washington with them. The group — and it is always a group consisting of water bearers, whisperers, hangers-on, spouses, and the press — operates like a miniature rolling capital. They have meetings, news conferences, telephone calls or wires from the office, and stay in touch with their pollsters. Instead of immersing themselves in the real world, they make an otherwise nice spot of ground totally surreal.

Look at New Hampshire during a presidential primary. Every inn becomes a media event, every doorbell an opinion poll, and every small town a microcosm of America. And in a few weeks the show folds. Hello, good-bye.

Covering a 1982 White House campaign trip to the Midwest, where Ronald Reagan was to stump for Illinois Representative Robert Michel, I watched as a corn field became a mass communications center. Telephones sprang fully formed out of the ground, camera and microphone wires spread across the land, and an army of reporters, advance staff, and Secret Service agents marched past hundreds of "real people" who stood behind ropes and barricades.

Nothing like mixing it up with the folks.

Walking into the field hefting a portable typewriter and a ten-pound press kit, I felt as though I had just landed. I wanted to say, "Hey, I'm a human being from Ohio and my father grew up working a farm," but there seemed to be a universe separating the people on either side of the barricades. We watched Reagan drive a new tractor around in a circle, took notes, took pictures, and then left as quickly as we had come, vanishing in a haze of bus fumes.

That night at a rally for Michel in the Peoria Civic Center, I stood under a spectator stand talking on a phone bank that had mysteriously grown out of a gymnasium floor and dictated a story to Boston, hundreds of miles away. Looking through the feet of some spectators, I could see Pat Boone on the stage in a white suit and Charlton Heston being introduced as "Chuck." Anybody who calls Moses "Chuck" in the heartland doesn't get out there enough.

The next day the President popped in and out of schools, rode back and forth to hotels, and eventually disappeared into the clouds with the rest of us behind him. And as we roared off, I know an Illinois farmer picked up a stray press release, looked into the horizon, and said more to himself than anyone in particular, "Who were those masked people?"

12

Reading
the Power Meter

THE BUSINESS OF THE DAY for people in Washington is trying to figure out how much political power they've got. That's why just about everybody in town has a power meter.

You don't move to Minneapolis without a good snow shovel. You don't hit New York City without a set of hefty locks on the car. And you don't hang up your shingle in the nation's capital without a top-of-the-line clout-checking system.

Most people in other parts of the country have never seen a power meter and probably never will unless they get really deep into national politics — knee-deep would probably do it. A power meter is not something politicians talk about on the evening news. It's personal. Write to your local senator and representative and inquire about their power meters and they'll send back a polite note referring you to the Department of Energy. Talking about how much power one has in Washington is cool. Talking about how much angst one goes through trying to figure out how much power one has in Washington is not cool. That's like balancing the checkbook at a lunch counter or stopping the poker game to count chips.

Power must be calculated in private: quietly, carefully, and constantly. With the Washington rumor mill operating continuously and new realities being created every few hours, this is no easy task. Yesterday's up is today's down and tomorrow's nowhere. A person can be a front-runner in the morning and on a train for the law practice back in New Jersey by the afternoon. Careers turn on whim and luck and the caprice of lightning bolts. It's not like the old days when power was power and empires shook with the wave of a hand. Attila the Hun, for instance, rarely sweat the polls. He knew who he was and what he had and where to get more. If he woke up one morning feeling a little insecure, he simply went out and ate a country for breakfast and regained his composure.

Politicians in America today would love to be able to do that, at least verbally, anyway, but can't. The only way they can gain knowledge of where they stand is through twitches and blips on a public opinion graph. It's all fine tuning — a twist of the dial to the right or left, no dramatic gestures, an inch of progress, maybe, on a good day, if the sun is shining and the numbers have been interpreted correctly. They flex their muscles in increments during committee meetings, stick a toe into the water here or hold a finger to the wind there, and constantly wonder what sort of impact they are having.

The power meter tells them. Available in a variety of sizes, including one small enough to fit into a briefcase, the little black box is ever at the ready to monitor a Washington career professional's exact position on the political compass.

This indispensable gadget for every political kitchen was invented by Richard Nixon in 1955. He was serving as vice president to Dwight Eisenhower back then and had time to tinker. Eisenhower had time to tinker, too, but preferred playing golf.

The system Nixon developed was crude by today's standards and consisted of a bank of radios, a light bulb, and an alarm clock. He had a half-dozen aides in a basement room of the White House listening to news shows around the country. The aides also received reports via walkie-talkie from a team of staff members on the street who were following Washington gossip. Every time Nixon's name was mentioned, the basement team pushed a button that lit a light bulb under the vice president's desk. If they did not receive confirmation of the signal within five minutes, they assumed their boss wasn't looking under his desk and pushed another button that activated an alarm clock in his bottom drawer. When he was out of the office, a special assistant was assigned to sit in the room and record the signals.

Word of Nixon's invention spread around town as word of everything spreads around town, and people found the idea irresistible, although nobody said so out loud, especially not the Democrats. Over the years the device became increasingly complex, with alarms and bulbs giving way to silicon chips, 256K RAMs, and three-color graph-writing capabilities. Today the equipment can be programmed to register just about any flutter in the political atmosphere and calibrate its impact on a particular individual. Power meters also usually come with an extensive support staff that includes pollsters, analysts, and consultants who are trained to interpret the numbers.

Although systems vary greatly with personal tastes and needs, the basic power meter is a small square computer that stands about two feet wide and two feet high and has a dozen wires trailing out of its back panel. Each wire is equipped with magnetized sensors that can be attached to a variety of information sources around the home or office — typically, the radio, television, videocassette recorder, telephone-answering machine, personal computer, and microwave oven. When the computer's power switch is activated, all the appliances being included in the reading click on, and the meter's synthesizer begins registering and computing electronic and atmospheric impulses relevant to the operator.

Current news reports on the radio and television are measured against old ones stored in the VCR for a sense of the politician's public image and how it is changing. Telephone calls are factored into the equation, particularly late-night calls from the White House and the Hill which indicate a person's indispensability within the Washington power matrix. Microwave oven use is tallied as an indicator of how much food the subject is warming up and gulping down alone at home as opposed to his or her getting out and eating in public where it counts. There is also a wire attached to a special windsock on the roof that gives the immediate direction of prevailing political winds and indicates whether they are likely to change. In addition, the meter's antenna can pick up rumor-mill rumblings within a two-mile radius and sort them into negative and positive gossip groups. All of this information is matched up with career-goal spread sheets stored in the computer. This tells the person how closely private ambitions are aligned with public perceptions of his or her job performance.

After processing the data from each of the information sources, the power meter does an analysis of a subject's Real Underlying Measurable Power, or RUMP, and Perceived Underlying Measurable Power, or PUMP. These readings appear in separate windows on the front of the machine, where needles indicate intensity on a scale of one to ten. In Washington PUMP, or perceived power, is a lot more important than RUMP because having other people think you're powerful gets more results than being powerful and not having anyone notice. Still, the RUMP reading is very important and needs to be taken regularly so that the person knows how much to bet in the poker game.

A third window, at the top of the power meter, produces a Profile Curve on a line graph that indicates whether a person's profile is high or low. Generally speaking, most politicians in Washington strive for a low profile with a quick surfacing every three or four weeks. They want to be known, but not for the wrong reasons, and the high profile is usually considered too risky. A person who is constantly making a splash is very likely to get the wrong people wet, and so the solid, steady profile line with regular high-publicity peaks is considered the safest way to go.

The machine is also equipped with an Image Indicator —
a rapidly rotating mirror that flashes colored lights correspond-
ing to current popularity. Red means people are hot, and blue
means they're not. Green means they're in transition, and
yellow means nobody cares. In addition, a beeper sounds to
rate a person's Momentum Potential, or how likely one would
be to win anything if one were running. The louder the beep,
the greater the chances of success in the election.

RUMP, PUMP, Profile Curve, Image Indicator, and
Momentum Potential are factored together for the bottom
line, or LUMP, Latest Updated Measurable Power, which is
printed out in the form of a brief one-page report that slides
through a slot on the side of the machine. After studying the
individual readings and discussing the printed report with key
aides by phone, a politician usually has enough of a grip on
things to get dressed in the morning and go to the office.

At work a new reading is immediately taken on the office
meter and compared with the home report. The office is, after
all, in another part of town, and the rumor mill and windsock
data may be different. Also, Xerox machine use is factored in,
and a sensor is attached to the office door to record the number of times people go in and out of the room. LUMPs are
taken every couple of hours during the day, and raw data are
fed into the machine after press conferences, meetings, working meals, media reports, and whatever else seems significant, which includes just about anything that happens in
Washington.

Naturally, while all this personal monitoring is going on,
aides are also keeping a close eye on the political fortunes of
the rest of the players in town. Simply tallying up your own
score in Washington is about as useful as taking your pulse
in an earthquake. The whole vast, ever-shifting landscape
must be constantly scrutinized for fissures, cracks, rumblings,
and new alignments on the horizon. When the *New York
Times* announces that there is "Much Flux in the Democratic
Firmament," everybody reads it, including the Republicans.

Firmaments do not flux alone. They affect other firmaments and cause meteor showers in career heavens for miles around. Likewise, when the *Washington Post* proclaims that "McFarlane's Hidden Hand Guides U.S. Foreign Policy," people outside the White House have to know exactly where that hand is hiding and how far down Pennsylvania Avenue he intends to push it.

The *Times* eventually told them in a May 26, 1985, Sunday magazine cover story that pictured the once-hidden-handed McFarlane with his arms boldly crossed, standing sternly in front of a misty blue background that made him appear to be ascending into the fluxing firmament. The headline read, "Taking Charge — The Rising Power of National Security Adviser Robert McFarlane." Seven months later, the ascending hidden hand was waving good-bye, as McFarlane resigned after clashes with other "take charge" types in the administration. Watching him go, the *Post* wrote, "Despite Inside Job, McFarlane Was an Outsider."

How quickly they forget.

People who are going places in Washington are either "rising," "emerging," or "expanding." The term "rising" is usually reserved for gray eminences who are held in awe because they are involved in matters very few people understand. "Emerging" people, on the other hand, tend to come from a stable of staffers who do support work for the gray eminences. They are the next generation struggling to be born, kicking their way out of the womb of power to stand tall on their own. They are watched very closely, particularly by the gray eminences, who don't want them standing too tall too fast and blocking the view from the top. In February 1985 when the *Times* spoke of "the emergence of Mr. Svahn," a thousand pairs of eyes narrowed sagely and a bit suspiciously, and a thousand lips formed the words, "Ah, yes. Svahn."

You remember Mr. Svahn. Good old John. He was over in the Social Security Administration for a while before he went to Health and Human Services and then on to the

White House, where he became chief domestic policy adviser, and "emerged."

Emergers should not be confused with "expanding" people. Expanders rest in the middle ground between emergers and rising gray eminences. When Washington speaks of someone as "emerging," that means no one is too sure whether the person will ever actually make it, but people want to go on record as having been aware of the possibility in case it happens. When someone's role is described as "expanding," it's certain that he or she has emerged in a big way and usually nobody likes it much.

In the spring of 1985 the papers announced that the White House communications director, Patrick J. Buchanan, was "expanding his domain." They described him as "testing his growing influence" and said he was "becoming the real power in the White House." Finally, he reached the ne plus ultra of expansionism when a "senior official" told the *Washington Post* that "Pat is pushing the President."

Now, it's a well-known fact that the goal of everybody hanging around the Oval Office doorway is to push the President. That's the whole idea of working there. Parents in political families all over America are looking at their children right now and saying, "Someday you may grow up to push the President." No doubt what that senior official was really thinking when he talked to the *Post* was, "Pat is pushing the President and it's my turn."

When Ronald Reagan went into the hospital for intestinal surgery in the summer of 1985, power meters around town were tuned to the Oval Office to see who would take charge without making it seem as though they were taking advantage of the presidential polyp. Vice President George Bush appeared to be hovering tentatively in the doorway, having been "assigned powers" one day and then "slipping back into a low-profile post" the next. White House Chief of Staff Donald T. Regan was said to be "more firmly in charge" and "consolidating his power," raising "concerns" among colleagues.

His assistant, Dennis Thomas, was being hailed as a "leading assistant" who was inching toward scheduling and personnel management duties, and quite possibly "emerging."

After a spate of these emergings, risings, and expansions occurs at the White House during a relatively short time span, one of two things is sure to follow — a power vacuum or a power shuffle. A power vacuum comes about when there are too many people pushing the President at once. A jam-up occurs at the Oval Office door and nothing can get in or out. The traditional time for the vacuum is two years into any administration's term, which is why it is also referred to as "the midterm crisis." It is similar to a mid-life crisis only not as long. The average Washington vacuum, or midterm crisis, lasts about two weeks, and word of it is leaked to the press by someone who hasn't been able to push the President for months.

The shuffle is by far the more exciting event because it involves changes in people's job titles. Whenever there is a title change anywhere in Washington, power meters go off the charts and sound the alarms. Staff meetings are called, strategy sessions are planned, and the troops hunker down over the organization charts to figure out who will be next and what it will mean.

This is extremely difficult, particularly the "what it will mean" part, as anyone who has ever read a government directory knows. The creation of job titles here almost equals the verbiage output and is just as confusing. Every millimeter of every rung of the career ladder has been carved into a bailiwick with a title and at least two assistants. A shift at the top of the ladder scatters bailiwicks all the way down the line and causes a lot of sleepless nights.

Say someone is reassigned to the post of special assistant to the secretary of transportation. That may sound fairly impressive until one looks on the roster and realizes one will be working next door to an executive assistant to the secretary of transportation, a deputy secretary, an associate deputy secretary, a special assistant to the deputy secretary, and a director of the executive secretariat.

There is so much assisting going on that very few people actually remember what the primary objectives of their organizations are anymore. In the State Department, for instance, there are assistant secretaries, assistant undersecretaries, deputy assistant secretaries, principal deputy assistant secretaries, senior deputy assistant secretaries, assistant coordinators, advisers, special advisers, senior advisers, officers in charge, liaisons, and through-put directors. Over in Congress the personnel maze wanders through legislative assistants, legislative directors, legislative strategists, executive assistants, administrative assistants, personal assistants, research assistants, chief counsels, general counsels, associate counsels, and assistant counsels. In the Department of Agriculture they even have confidential assistants as well as associate chiefs.

So, who's on first? Probably all of the above, or at least they think they are, which makes for that delightful atmosphere of camaraderie evident in the Washington work place. To gain a clue about who is in charge, people keep careful track of the perks — noting the size of an office, the type of furniture, whether there's a window and if it looks out on the Capitol or a trash dumpster. The higher up the ladder people go, the larger their desk tops and the richer the wood. Of course, this is patently ridiculous, since flat surfaces are not really needed in the upper echelons. They are needed at the bottom, where the paper is summarily sent to be sorted and processed by the poor, suffering GS-6's who sit buried under it at little metal tables with cheapo in-baskets.

At any rate, big desks, big chairs with arms, banks of file cabinets, pictures, plants, rugs, and a government car indicate that the field director for special projects has it all over the senior executive associate deputy. Unless, that is, the senior executive associate deputy happens to be in an office closer to the cabinet secretary or the senator or the President.

Proximity to the top is the ultimate arbiter of power. You

can have a carpeted suite with piped-in music and a view of the river in the most modern building in town, but it'll mean zilch when pitted against any cubby in the west wing of the White House. That's the section closest to the Oval Office, and as Michael K. Deaver, former deputy chief of staff, told the *New York Times* in a March 5, 1985, story, "People will kill to get an office in the west wing."

"I mean, they don't care where it is," Deaver continued. "You'll see people working in closets, tucked back in a corner, rather than taking a huge office with a fireplace in the Executive Office Building, just so they can say they work in the west wing."

You have to know what's important around here, not what makes sense. You also have to watch the people exiting those west wing offices as closely as you watch those ascending to them. Slippage down the ladder of power is considered every bit as important as rising, emerging, and expanding. After all, if one's political fortunes are tied to a biggie who is being eased out — or "losing influence," as they say — one's power equation could be definitely hurting. Signs of decline must be carefully noted and fed into the power-meter computer. For instance, has a person been moved from the "A" meeting list in the organization to the "B" list? Is he or she making excuses about not being included because of a "sudden trip overseas"? Are there headlines in the papers that say things like, "Whither Burt?" or "Kirkpatrick Postpones Session with Reagan — Her Future Was to Have Been Discussed," or "Packwood's Role in Tax Overhaul Central but Uncertain"?

That last one must have sent a few shudders through the legislative-assistant ranks on the Hill. There it was in black and white for anybody who had hitched his or her wagon to the Republican senator's star — their man was "issuing conflicting statements." And a highly placed Treasury Department official was writing him off with devastating bluntness, saying, "Of all the people who could screw it up, chances are it will be him."

Not nice, and not a good day to be wearing a "Packwood for President" button.

There was some equally tense adjusting of the power meters in the Treasury and Commerce departments on April 25, 1985, when the *Times* told all in a turf battle story that ran under the headline, "Weinberger Wins One." It described the defense secretary's "skirmish" with Treasury Secretary James A. Baker III and Commerce Secretary Malcolm Baldrige over who would get to "devise the strategy and tactics" for the trip Baldrige was taking to Moscow.

"Mr. Baker and Mr. Baldrige wanted the preparations for the trip handled by the new Economic Policy Council headed by Mr. Baker," the paper reported. "But Mr. Weinberger, who is not a regular member of this council and goes to its meetings only by invitation, wanted the trip arranged through the National Security Council, where he is one of the principal officials."

On such infinitesimal tugs of war do political fortunes hang in this city. And the spoils of the game keep going back and forth and back and forth, with the Bakers and the Baldriges regaining their inch of ground only to give it up again to the Weinbergers a few meetings down the road.

In 1983 the *Post* ran a story on Secretary of State George Shultz's dwindling inches, titled "Shultz No Longer Perceived as Driving Force in Foreign Policy." Two years later in about the same spot the paper ran one that read, "Shultz Firmly in Command — 'He Just Keeps on Coming,' Observer Says."

So, there's slippage and there's slippage, if you know what I mean, just as there is emerging and emerging, and anybody who takes it seriously deserves to do both at the same time.

Which reminds me, has anyone seen Mr. Svahn lately?

13

Seen Any
Good Issues Lately?

THE CONGRESSMAN sounded as though his pet goldfish had died.

It was the spring of 1983, the nuclear weapons freeze resolution had just passed the House after being a national issue for months, and he was one of the congressional leaders backing the movement. Logic would suggest that he'd be skipping around his office singing "Happy Days Are Here Again," but this is Washington. His voice had a flat quality and didn't come close to matching the enthusiasm he'd had when he spoke so forcefully for so long on the need to get the resolution passed.

"So you must be popping champagne over there," I said naively during a phone interview.

"Sure," he said, and then there was a silence followed by a sigh. He hesitated, gave a short laugh, and said, "There's just one thing. Now what do I do?"

The problem had obviously been distressing him so much that he didn't care if he was telling a reporter about it. In fact, he seemed desperate for some sort of media advice.

"What's next?" he asked. "Is it Central America? Should I take a trip down there? What's your sense of this?"

Let the record show that this is the only time anyone in power has ever sought my sage counsel.

"Gee," I said. "You got me."

Sitting at the other end of the phone with my mouth open, I remember thinking that this had to be some sort of aberration in the process caused by the congressman's being a bit of a nut. But I have since learned that while he may have been a little more panicked than most, he was merely verbalizing what every other elected official in Washington is thinking twenty-four hours a day: please, Lord, send me an issue that will get me on the *Today* show.

The congressman had been to the *Today* show and had seen the presidency. They have all seen the presidency here. It's the great universal mirage shimmering on the issues landscape. Hit the right cause, the logic goes, and you can catapult yourself smack into the Oval Office, or at least the Senate.

The average American living in a normal environment doesn't view issues this way. Out there, an issue is usually connected with rightness or wrongness, passion, outrage, and moral choice. People in Omaha do not look at the charts, hold a strategy session, and then announce with all the animation of a mushroom: "We think the corruption issue will work well for us."

That's what Democratic leaders were telling the press here during the 1984 presidential campaign when they thought they would benefit from Ronald Reagan's problems with indicted Labor Secretary Raymond Donovan and others in the administration. It had been worked out on paper, you see. The power meter had been consulted and the numbers were right. The pollsters had produced a consensus and it was now official—the corruption issue will work well for us.

Kind of gives you an idea why Walter Mondale lost.

In Washington an issue does not present itself in a blinding flash of truth. It's more like a package of freeze-dried mashed potatoes. It sits on the shelf with a load of other packets until the time is right for breaking it open, adding water, and whipping the hell out of it.

This is called "shaping the issue." The activity provides full-time employment for hundreds of people with advanced degrees, and if it was done for pay anywhere else in the country it would be considered goldbricking. But here, people known as "issues managers," "issues coordinators," and "issues facilitators" proudly relate how they plumped up arms control for the senator or got the representative out front on farm subsidies by calling a press conference, scheduling a hearing, or writing a provocative speech for their boss to give before anybody else did.

Timing is everything in these matters. A person cannot simply take a packet off the shelf and add water just because one feels like having potatoes. The staff must decide upon the proper moment for the issue to be "identified," or disclosed, which occurs after the issue has been properly "shaped." The staff works for weeks or months, adding water, whipping, and molding the raw material into proper form so that a politician can parade it in front of a television camera at just the right moment and say, "Look what I found, and it's all mine." If an issue is identified too early, it will be ignored; too late, and the boss could appear to be tagging along instead of leading.

Once a politician has identified an issue, staff people become very proprietary about it and act as though the senator owns arms control or has purchased the environment with an appearance on a panel. Conversely, they can get rather testy when someone broaches a subject that has not been disclosed by their office, or at least not by them.

"That's not my issue," they snip, and it has the same tone as, "I don't do windows."

These people have life carved up into topics of concern and unconcern. They meet other people at parties, shake hands, smile mechanically, and ask with what they must assume is an expansive display of interest in their fellow human beings: "What are your issues?"

This is the Washington career equivalent of "What is your major?" and it elicits the same stimulating response it did when people asked it back in college. A reporter who spent a year on a congressional fellowship told me that when he was asked that question at his first Hill party, he became flip and irreverent but no one noticed.

"I just want to take care of a few niggling problems," he told an earnest, intense staffer. "I'd like to pay off the national debt, clear up the balance of trade problem, and end inflation forever."

"The senator would support you on that," replied the aide without so much as a twitch.

Placing his tongue more firmly in cheek, the reporter went on to say that once those bits of business were out of the way, he hoped to push for cutting off diplomatic relations with Japan because he felt America had never really gotten even for Pearl Harbor.

A momentary wrinkle creased the brow of the earnest, intense aide, who then said quickly, "I can't speak for him on that. You'll have to talk to our committee people."

And you can bet that there is a committee person into whose bailiwick the matter would fall. You can also bet that talking to this person would be like doing a scene from *The Stepford Wives*.

Real emotions are confiscated at the border here. Living in Washington is, as a friend says, like living backstage at a theater. It's all blue smoke and mirrors, and gut-wrenching feelings are contrived and timed for maximum effect. You see the chicken wire holding up the mountain and the tape covering the cracks on the wall of the set. You watch the tech crew pull ropes, hit the lights, and open trap doors, and hear the cast constantly discussing how best to play the role.

People have become so used to this coolly considered display of public passion that they think of it as reality—interesting reality, even. In May 1985 Craig L. Fuller, chief of staff to George Bush, talked with the *New York Times* about how the Vice President was strategizing for the 1988 election. "There is every desire for us to continue to play a supporting role, but also to begin to carve out some areas where the Vice President's direct involvement can either raise the visibility of an issue or where he can be engaged in trying to seek solutions that would be consistent with what the Administration is trying to do."

Fuller must be a riot at the dinner table.

"What did you do at the office today, Daddy?"

"Oh, I raised the visibility of some issues and engaged in high-power solution seeking."

"Wow. Next time can I watch?"

After the bombings of abortion clinics in the D.C. area, the *Washington Post* ran a story that began not with straight reportage on the loss of property but with the news that Mayor Marion Barry was "staking out a leading position on the issue of violence." Three paragraphs into the story the paper reported what the mayor had to say about the bombings, but obviously the big news for Washington was that the old boy had gotten hold of some strategic political ground and was using it skillfully.

Hey, everybody, watch the mayor take center stage and express outrage. Not bad.

In a story on young lawyers coming to work for members of Congress, the *New York Times* asked one new recruit to explain why he found the Hill exciting and inspiring. "You open the paper," he said, "and there are the issues we're working on and sometimes shaping."

O rash, impetuous Youth!

Can you imagine what would have happened if these types had been around for the American Revolution? The bright young aide would have gone in to John Adams with three opinion polls and a chart, looked at him studiously, and said, "I think we should emphasize the fairness issue, sir, and go national with a statement on the Stamp Act."

Sure they played politics back then, just as all politicians play politics. After all, these were the folks who worked a fast deal to put the nation's capital in swamp water. But the issue pile seemed to be a lot smaller two hundred years ago, and the freeze-dried packet hadn't been invented yet. There were a couple or three good, solid problems: was the country ready for independence; who should do what about slavery; and what would happen to three-cornered hats if the Indians hung our hair out to dry in the woods that night. These were issues that needed to be solved immediately and were so enormous that everybody could get a chunk of them and be "out front."

But today there are thousands of issues, and resolving them is the last thing anybody wants. A politician with a resolved issue is like a unicyclist with a flat. Hence the depression of the nuclear freeze leader. Once his cause had passed in the House, he couldn't very well stand out in the hall all day and shout warnings to the Senate. He had to find another issue. Fast.

And it had to be big. Very big. A veritable quandary and a quagmire of bigness. To be considered an issue, a matter must grapple with the cosmic — things like nuclear war, the declining quality of education in America, immigration law reform, intergalactic relations, and crime in the streets.

A sewer bill does not dramatic-issue material make, although politicians certainly push for their local sewer bills and their grants to home-state colleges and their highway aid. But the truth is, nobody ever got on *Meet the Press* standing tall for public works legislation. That stuff is routine maintenance—necessary, rewarding in its way, but not the reason people go into politics.

People go into politics so they can talk, and with the right issue they can talk forever. They can haul out the heavy vocabulary and dramatic arm gestures and shout, "It is imperative that we move the country forward," or "We are foundering on the dangerous shoals of complacency," or "It is our duty to do the will of the American people." That one always sounds good if you're sitting in a crowd listening, unless you stop and try to remember exactly when the last time was that you had your will done in Washington. (How about your laundry and dry cleaning?)

Whenever a politician talks about "the will of the American people," it's usually a sure sign that he's got himself a can't-miss issue that can be explained in forty-five seconds and will look good on television.

The nuclear freeze was a definite can't-miss issue in 1983, a politician's dream, and I say that as someone whose heart is with the movement and who has a lot of respect for its organizers. But the call for the United States and the Soviet Union to negotiate a mutual, verifiable freeze on the production, deployment, and testing of nuclear weapons was simple, emotional, and probably impossible, given the complexities of the Russian mind and of arms control. It was a populist idea that swept the country precisely because of its simplicity, and the politicians who latched on to it did so primarily for that reason. And it should be noted that the opposition latched on with equally simple and emotional counterarguments, by insisting that the commies would march into New York City if a freeze was on the table.

The point is, nobody was going on the tube with a tedious, complex explanation saying that both sides had part of the answer and that to understand why would probably take the next three weeks. That's not good show biz, and issues are show biz — short, snappy routines designed to capture the most media coverage in the shortest possible time.

When a spokesman for the Center for National Security Studies called to push a story on CIA involvement in Nicaragua, he did not give me an in-depth analysis of U.S. intelligence gathering in third world countries. Nor did he try to appeal to the supposed journalistic quest for truth. He just said simply, "We think it's a very good issue and that it's going to take off." The implication to me was, "And you can be in on the ground floor." A reporter who writes about an issue when it is first "identified" or, as is often the case, who causes it to be made public is accorded almost as much prestige as the politician associated with the disclosure.

The goal of both journalists and politicians is to see their particular issue "take off." That means it goes beyond the realm of routine shaping and identification and is elevated to superstar status. It is no longer merely a good, solid little issue, but a brush fire of an idea that becomes almost as exciting as a Washington rumor.

A few words are spoken here, a couple of columns are written there, the *Post* does a three-part series, there's wind of a documentary, the hearings start, and suddenly the whole town is incapable of talking about anything but hazardous waste dumps or the deficit or the Middle East. One single blazing topic becomes the lightning rod of the hour, drawing fire and heat and shedding very little light. It will have intense attention for anywhere from two weeks to a month, and every politician in town will feel compelled to grab a part of it for his or her own, even at the risk of appearing to be a follower. The issues-management folk are driven into a frenzy as they rip open packets, spill water all over the place, and blow fuses trying to figure out how to make their boss appear to be saying something unique when everybody has already said it six ways from Sunday.

Very often they will turn to Hollywood for help. Their boss may not have anything original to say, but he or she will get on the evening news by saying it while standing next to a movie star. They bring former *M*A*S*H* actor Mike Farrell out for arms control or call in Stacy Keach to talk about cocaine addiction. In May 1985 when the plight of the farmer was the issue of the moment, a Democratic task force on agriculture lined up Jane Fonda, Sissy Spacek, and Jessica Lange, who had all starred in movies about rural life. Camera crews were fighting for space in the packed hearing room and the actresses cried on cue.

If issues organizers can't get a movie star, they try for whoever is on the cover of *Time* or *Newsweek*. The attorney for New York subway vigilante Bernhard Goetz was down here when Goetz was a front-pager, and so was Cathleen Webb, the woman who recanted a rape charge in 1985. During the

Environmental Protection Agency scandal in the early Reagan years, just about every committee on the Hill that had ever had a passing nod with environmental issues tried to call up EPA Administrator Anne Burford. If they couldn't get Burford, they announced that they had launched an investigation of Burford, or that they were calling Burford's key assistants, or that they would be reading Burford's memos. There were so many people employed to investigate Burford that when she finally left office, there was a drop in the GNP.

It will be the same if the defense contract overcharge scandals ever sink back into oblivion. That one has been a sure-fire issue for anybody who has enough wind to huff. People just pick an item and yell. Representative Berkley Bedell got the $400 hammer, Senator William Roth got the $600 toilet seat, somebody else got the $695 ashtray, and you can run for office on just about anything else in the Pentagon supply cabinet.

Once an issue has "taken off" it is unavoidable, even if you're trying to duck it. The week of April 15, 1985, was Nicaragua week, and there was no escape. Contra rebels had the town covered, trying to convince anyone who would listen that the Congress should pass the aid package. Committees that hadn't been south of Atlanta were suddenly on top of Central America. The Senate Subcommittee on Alcoholism and Drug Abuse figured out a way to get a piece of the action by having a session on illegal drug trafficking from . . . guess which country?

I was working on a story about First Ladies, which had absolutely nothing to do with Nicaragua, and yet I wound up having lunch with a Contra. When the bureau chief walked in and said he had a rebel coming over for sandwiches, I automatically signed up and took notes. Afterward I went back to my desk and started writing. It wasn't until the third paragraph that I realized I had nothing to say.

This stuff is contagious. It is also ridiculous and strangely necessary because not to be "up on the issues" in Washington is to die. Go to a social gathering without being able to offer scintillating commentary on Nicaragua during Contra week, and you'll be relegated to the pretzel bowls in the outer rooms. I always feel as though I should take a crib sheet to these fests. Even with the Contra lunch, to this day whenever Central America comes up at a party I have to close my eyes, concentrate very hard, and say to myself, "Okay, we support the rebels in Nicaragua, and we back the government in El Salvador."

If anybody starts talking about Honduras, I head for the john.

I feel like the sea captain in that old joke about the ship. It seems the captain was driving his crew crazy with his ritual of going to his cabin three times a day, opening a locked chest, taking out a yellow sheet of paper, and meditating upon it. He refused to explain what he was doing, so the crew, unable to stand the mystery any longer, sneaked into the captain's quarters one night and broke open the chest. They pulled out the yellow paper and eagerly read the secret, which was written in bold black letters: "Right is starboard, left is port."

There are vast spaces of ignorance that one doesn't want to admit to out loud in the nation's capital — for instance, that one isn't too sure where the Falkland Islands are, or how the Supreme Court voted on school prayer the last time around, or exactly what the House did yesterday or even if it was in session. Nothing kills an erudite conversation about a powerful personage who is obviously going places quite like a hesitant little voice from the sidelines asking, "Is that guy in the Senate or the House?"

During a news conference on I forget what, in front of the Capitol, I walked up to a man I thought was another reporter and asked him if anybody from New England was going to speak at the gathering. He said *he* would be. He was a congressman from Connecticut.

I had no idea what his issues were. And given the speed with which they change, maybe he didn't, either.

"Americans have such a short attention span," a man from

Germany once told me during an interview. "There is a lack of continuity here that is very unsettling to a foreigner."

It can be unsettling to the natives, too. In fact, I'd be willing to bet that Washington has unsettled Americans in every state of the Union for decades. But that's not to say I'd want to make an issue of it.

14

Never-Never Land

I DON'T WANT TO upset anyone, but the average mental age of the people running our government is about fifteen. On a good day.

Washington may look fairly sophisticated from the tour bus windows, and people sound pretty grown up when they make speeches on television, but hang out with this crowd for a while and you'll wonder why John Belushi never ran for Congress.

Actually he did. He goes by the name of Robert Dornan here, and when he hits the floor of the House, he does everything except yell "food fight!" — but more on him later.

I wasn't always this irreverent. I had respect. At first I stood in awe, as any new kid at a new school stands in awe of the other kids, and figured that if anything juvenile was happening, it was me. If Representative Barney Frank was taking a nutty on the phone, I had obviously violated some code and pushed his equanimity to the wall. If White House aide Richard Darman was accusing me of trying to blackmail him, then I must have acted like an undiplomatic jerk — as opposed to a diplomatic jerk.

It was only after living here for a couple of years — staring hard into the bathroom mirror and meditating on the great questions of new schools and life — that I decided I was not a jerk. After all, I had not been a jerk in Boston, so why would a person metamorphose into one upon crossing the Mason-Dixon line? No, I really had seen Representative Silvio Conte wearing a pig mask at a press conference, and this was the big frat house in the sky.

The sophomoric continually clashes with the chic here, and visions of a gang in short pants keep inching into my mind's eye alongside the tuxedos. It's something I have come to think of as "the Peter Pan syndrome." Washington, for all its talk of being the citadel of wisdom, leadership, and power in the Western world, is actually a colony of lost boys.

I say boys even though they let girls play now, because the essential character of the city is, was, and most likely always will be stereotypically male. This does not mean women aren't doing well here or that they haven't adapted beautifully to the foot-stomping, us-against-them, knock-three-times-and-say-the-secret-password atmosphere.

They have grasped the essential truth that Washington is a clubhouse. A series of clubhouses really, each one working toward its own end and dedicated to being exclusive. The Senate is a club, the House another, the White House a third; the city's law firms and courts each its own; and the squash, tennis, and running groups also form their own societies. Then there are clubs within clubs where senior members separate themselves from juniors, personal staff from committee staff, home-towners from out-of-staters, White House west wingers from the less favored workers in the executive office buildings, and support personnel from the professionals. Only certain people in the office go out to lunch together or are invited to the baseball game. Only certain people share the inside information.

Clubs form instantaneously at the slightest excuse for some kind of cohesion. I remember a press secretary to former Massachusetts Representative Jim Shannon sending out memos to

New England reporters announcing the congressman's new unlisted home telephone number. Most people who get unlisted home telephone numbers do so precisely because they never want them announced in memos to the press, but in Washington the purpose of privacy is to create exclusivity. The press secretary felt exclusive, Shannon presumably felt exclusive, and the reporters with the memo could jump up and down and shout to their counterparts at other papers, "I'm in the Jim Shannon Club and you're not."

"Oh, yeah?"

"Yeah."

"Prove it."

"I can dial the hot line anytime I want."

"Big whoop."

"So's your old man."

And so it goes.

I helped organize a club in Washington once. It died.

We were about a dozen strong and called ourselves the New England Reporters Group, or NERG. That could explain why it died. We tried to model ourselves after the Sperling Breakfast, a Washington institution founded by the *Christian Science Monitor*. They pulled in people from the White House; we were going to concentrate on New England's movers and shakers. Inexplicably, our first guest was Senator Ernest Hollings from South Carolina. Actually, not so inexplicably. The presidential election was coming up, and Hollings was running and talking to anybody. He arrived late, talked about what he'd do if he were President, did an imitation of a Boston accent, and left.

We had a meeting after he'd gone and decided to try harder next time. Obviously, we needed big names. If we didn't pull prime New England talent into our exclusive club, nobody would care that they hadn't been invited to join. We decided to shoot for a session with House Speaker Tip O'Neill, and I was elected to extend the invitation, since the *Boston Globe* was the largest paper in New England and presumably had the most clout. Unfortunately, the closest thing I had to clout was Jim Shannon's unlisted phone number.

I could have gone to the clout mavens in my bureau who were charter members of the Tip O'Neill Club and begged for assistance, but I decided to blaze an independent trail with NERG. I had my club; they had theirs.

I called O'Neill's office solo, was shunted from press secretary to aide to appointments secretary, and told to write O'Neill a letter. I sat down, wrote the letter, and waited. This was in midsummer. By fall there had been no answer, and I decided independence wasn't working. I went to a colleague who said he just happened to be having dinner with the Speaker that night and he'd see what he could do.

The next morning he came into my office looking solicitous and said he was sorry, but O'Neill was really busy and wouldn't have time to get back to me until sometime in January or February.

I had come to Washington to learn how the place worked, and this was one of my first and most valuable lessons: don't mess with other people's clubs because you'll screw up your own. Hey, if you could have dinner with O'Neill anytime you wanted, how hard would you try to book him at another table?

The place reminded me of Cleveland. I grew up in Cleveland, on San Diego Avenue on the city's west side, with a bunch of kids who had a clubhouse. We refused to play with the kids from the next block because they were from Mars. They'd straggle over, stand at the edge of the lawn and gawk, and we'd tell them to get lost and go find their own clubhouse. They were the Beach Street kids and we were the San Diego Avenue kids. It was as simple as that.

I think Washington is like this because the two professions that dominate the town — politics and journalism — don't ever require their practitioners to grow up. That's the appeal of going into either field. That's certainly why I signed up. As a journalist, I could stand on the sidelines of life and point, be an arbiter of truth and justice, never have to actually get up and test any of the theories, and go write about something else whenever I got bored. Not bad for a week's pay.

Most journalists I've known in other cities freely admit to this, which is essentially being mature about being immature, if that makes any sense. But in Washington journalists think they're important grown-ups, as do politicians. Both hit the confetti trail with a sense of duty and that look children get when they are trying to be very adult or when the captain of the high school debate team is going to make that big point in the tri-state regionals.

Politicians are in the "love me, I'm wonderful" business. They are the center of attention, wave their hands and make promises, wear silly hats, stay up all night at conventions, and expect to be taken seriously. Washington reporters take them seriously for the most part, following them on press planes that look like flying romper rooms. People run up and down the aisles on these flights, get all the booze they can drink, and rush for the door as the plane lands. It's total chaos that reporters don't see as chaos because they are covering the President, or the senator, or the candidate. They and the politicians they cover live life in the present and in the air, literally. Their marriages and families are on hold somewhere far away. They are full of the agenda, following the schedule over which they have no control, running, filing, speaking, getting the instant gratification of the cheers or the byline, going to bed late and waking up early so they can prove themselves all over again.

And when these two groups go at each other, they often sound like children fighting over toys. During the TWA hostage crisis in June 1985, White House spokesman Larry Speakes and reporters did battle over the word "crisis." Speakes said "crisis" was the media's, not his, description of the situation, and reporters pushed to know what word he'd use. The following exchange is from the White House transcript of the press briefing:

SPEAKES: That's a foolish, elementary and simplistic
    question.
REPORTER: Well, you raised that now. You just raised it.
SPEAKES: Well, I never used the word. Have I called it a
    crisis?
REPORTER: Do you consider it a crisis?
REPORTER: What do you call it — an incident? A diversion?
    Entertainment?
SPEAKES: It is certainly an incident . . .
REPORTER: Not a crisis.
REPORTER: Is it a crisis?
SPEAKES: Do I call it a crisis? That is a foolish, simplistic
    and elementary question.
REPORTER: You were the one who brought it up.
SPEAKES: No I didn't.
REPORTER: Yes you did.
SPEAKES: I did not. You . . .
REPORTER: You did . . .

So much for the rich exchange of ideas and the deep, probing colloquies between public officials and the press.

I have a feeling that very few people participating in this
dialogue considered it ridiculous. They were too busy being
indignant. Indignation is a full-time job for a lot of people
around here. So is outrage. People huff and puff and try to
blow each other's clubhouses down for the better part of the
day. They talk in terms of sports and battle analogies: being
on the team, winning one for the Gipper, losing and gaining
ground. Democratic Senator Edward Kennedy and Republican Senate Majority Leader Robert Dole have a daily debate
on CBS radio called *Face Off*. Rivals are continually charging,
mounting an attack, or receiving a stinging attack. One of my
favorite such descriptions appeared in the *Washington Post*
on April 26, 1985, under the headline "GOP Senators Dealt
a Setback":

"Senate Republican leaders got off to a shaky start yesterday in their push for a quick symbolic victory in the battle

over deficit reductions as they backed away from a showdown to avoid defeat at the hands of Democrats and GOP dissenters."

Half the fun of playing tin soldiers is getting the action — or inaction, as the case may be — covered by somebody playing war correspondent.

Which brings us back to Robert Dornan, who is never short on excitement. In the spring of 1985 the California Republican grabbed hold of New York Congressman Thomas Downey's tie and wouldn't let go because he felt the Democrat was soft on defense. A couple of months later he went on another rampage against the doves, shouting at Oregon Democrat Les AuCoin, "You're for absolutely nothing. You voted for nothing in your life for defense. You sit up here with your mouth dripping spleen and bile."

Sounds like a Stephen King movie.

So does the chain scene, which never actually took place but had been threatened by conservatives who were ticked off about a contested Indiana congressional race. After two hundred hours of debate and three recounts, the House voted to seat the Democratic instead of the Republican contender. House Republicans announced they were going to chain themselves to their seats in protest. They opted for a mass walkout instead, probably because they couldn't find enough chain or figure out where to put it. Also, if one of their number tied all of them in their seats, then he would be odd man out and have nobody to tie him up.

"It's a tribal thing," House Majority Whip Tom Foley told *Newsweek* when he was interviewed about the walkout. "Everybody's got to put on the blanket and march around the campfire. And no matter how moderate you are, this is a chance to rip open your shirt and show there is a big 'R' there."

Your elected representatives at work.

In 1984 a group of about a dozen conservatives known as "the right-wing guerrillas" monopolized the opening and closing sessions of the House with attacks on liberals, given solely for the benefit of the C-Span cable TV audience. The chamber was empty; nobody cared. At one point Tip O'Neill called for the cameras to pan the empty seats, and the conservatives took offense at what they felt was unwarranted editorial comment, setting off a debate that raged for months.

And when politicians aren't staging protests that waste time, they're suing each other. In that contested Indiana-seat fracas, the Republican contender, Richard McIntyre, sued the Democratic-controlled House for not giving him the election. Representative Guy Vander Jagt of Michigan has sued Speaker O'Neill and others because he feels the ratio of Republicans to Democrats on committees is unfair, and Representative Robert Walker of Pennsylvania has sued the House and the Senate to stop members from revising their remarks before they are printed in the *Congressional Record*.

If the Congress can't play nice, I think their mothers should come and take them home. But they won't. Petulance is considered more or less a virtue in the nation's capital. It is catered to, rewarded, and stroked. The temper fit is expected by many staff members who see themselves as whipping boys for the hyper boss. The fingers are snapped, the orders barked, and four aides trip over themselves to do the bidding of the great one.

The public image becomes so all-consuming that officials lose sight of themselves in immediate, one-on-one situations — which can create some very bizarre exchanges. In the spring of 1984 I called Richard Darman at the White House for a story on Elliot Richardson, who was running for the Senate in Massachusetts. Darman had worked for Richardson and was considered one of his protégés. I spent a week or so trying to get through to him and an aide finally conveyed the message that Darman would have no comment.

"Gee, that's strange that he'd have no comment," I said. "It'll look odd in the article."

When Darman finally called back, he was furious and asked who I thought I was, trying to blackmail him with threats about what I planned to publish. After a tense five or ten minutes, he calmed down and realized he was talking to somebody from NERG and not the mad blackmailer. He also had a lot of insightful things to say about Elliot Richardson, none of which I could print because Darman was at odds with the right wingers supporting Reagan, and he felt they'd get on his case for supporting a liberal Republican.

Now, it seems to me that a lot of time and frustration could have been avoided if Darman had just gotten on the phone and explained things the first time I'd called. I realize I'm not on the tippy top of his call-back list, but still, creating a scene — caused once again by overactive egos and the fear of reprisals from the club — somehow lessened the thrill I might have felt talking to an aide to the President of the United States.

The Reagan administration has had more than its share of chest-thumping scene makers do their thing over the years: former Interior Secretary James Watt, who eventually insulted every minority group in the book; U.S. Information Agency Director Charles Wick, who taped telephone conversations in his office without telling the callers, and who is said to be obsessive about things like color-coded files; and Barbara Honegger, a special assistant in the Justice Department, who wore a rabbit suit at a Reagan rally and wrote a guest editorial in the *Washington Post* attacking the President's policies toward women. She eventually left town angry at being shut out of the inner circle and claiming that she was the only person in the White House who "saw the whole picture." At last check she was in California writing a musical about the Reagan administration. It is based on *The Wizard of Oz.*

It's very easy to go nuts here. No doubt about it. Closed clubhouses make for paranoia, and people regularly assume that whoever they are talking to is from the rival gang and about to aim for the jugular. Usually they are right. The atmosphere reminds me of a poster a friend has in her office: "Just because you're paranoid doesn't mean they're not out to get you." This can be very unsettling to a newcomer who walks around town assuming he or she is going to have sane, rational dealings with people.

I remember the first time I wrote about Massachusetts Congressman Barney Frank. I thought I was paying him a great compliment when I relayed an anecdote in which he was said to have cooperated with his fellow congressmen by moving things along on a House floor vote instead of taking a lot of time to yell and scream about an issue he knew was a loser anyway. Such maturity is rare in politics, I thought to myself, and should be published. The day the article appeared, Frank was on the phone yelling and screaming over his issue, which he said he never dropped because he wasn't the kind of guy who dropped an issue once he got his teeth into it, and who did I think I was, making him look like an idiot in front of his constituents. He seemed to be convinced that I'd done it on purpose. The more I tried to explain how cool I thought he'd been about his floor vote, the hotter he got. I honestly think he would have felt better if I'd said I'd gone after him hammer and tongs and was out to send him back to the Massachusetts legislature.

Much of this hyper behavior is conscientiousness — wanting the voters to know that the job is being done well — which is admirable. But a lot of it is also something else, which isn't admirable and should go away.

There is a Peck's Bad Boy quality to it that says, "How outrageous can I be?" and "The more outrageous I am the better press I'll get." That's what makes Silvio Conte put on funny suits. He once appeared in an exterminator's outfit with plastic cockroaches glued to his shoulders to promote a new bug killer made by a company in his district. He also wore a yachtsman's outfit complete with captain's hat and signal-flag insignia to a House subcommittee hearing to push his bill calling for boat owners to pay fees in an effort to offset Coast Guard costs. Representative Gerry Studds, chairman of the Coast Guard subcommittee and an opponent of the bill, wore yellow fisherman's rain gear and opened the meeting by sounding a foghorn.

Ohio Senator Howard Metzenbaum once spoke at a hearing on proposed cuts in military pensions while standing next to a stack of boxes taller than he was, to demonstrate how many names would be cut from the rolls if the ax fell.

Why do they act like kids? Because the kids with the cameras and the notebooks eat it up.

Why do they speed down the street in long black stretch limos with flags flying? Because it's fun. The dignitaries traveling from point A to point B do not really need to run red lights. No, the reason they speed is because they like to speed. They like to watch the world go by through one-way glass and shout "Wheee!" to themselves. If I had access to a limo and a police escort I'd probably love it, too.

A lot of these people zipping around in their limos are usually dressed up. Why? Because they never got enough of playing dress-up as kids. So now their tuxedos and black dresses are a mark of adulthood. They've been invited. They're on the list, in the club. And there are so many of them out in the streets every night that I sometimes think the national bird should be the penguin instead of the eagle.

A survey by the National Institute on Alcohol Abuse and Alcoholism in 1983 showed that Washington, D.C., had the highest alcohol consumption rate in the country — 5.22 gallons per year per person versus the national average of 2.69 gallons per year per person.

Party, party, party. Just like college. The drinking drives a lot of people to shrinks, and because the couch business is so good, there are supposed to be more of them here than anywhere else in the country.

Washington is a great place to hide from yourself, to adopt a persona and be somebody else who always looks busy and important and admired. And like Peter Pan and the boys living out there beyond the first star to the right, they believe it is the only place in the universe to be, and they have no intention of returning to Earth anytime soon.

15

The Fat Man
and His Friends

THE FAT MAN is the meanest waiter in Washington, and
I have lunch at his place a couple of times a week.

Why do I have lunch at his place? Because it feels so good
when I stop. The Fat Man is sullen, tough, rude, big and bad,
but he is real. He is a solid wall against which to pound a fist,
a rock in an otherwise squishy terrain where the line between
friends and enemies changes with the political tides. The Fat
Man does not change. He offers no pretentions, no politicking,
no carefully worded press statement, no waving and working
the crowd, and no strategizing. He doesn't care who votes for
him. He doesn't rhapsodize over the béarnaise sauce, wax
obsequious about people having nice days, or ask if everything
is all right here. He knows how everything is. He's been in the
kitchen and seen it cooking. He just brings out that not-so-
great food, never pretends it is anything more, and quietly
and simply hates your face.

The Fat Man never yells. He doesn't have to. One look, one
squint from the pale, ice-water blue eyes, one slight twitch of
his jowly cheek muscle and you know it's time to shut up and
eat. New to the place, I once mentioned to him that my
hamburger bun was cold and asked if he could please put it
in the microwave.

The hulking shadow fell across the table. He leaned down — not smiling, not frowning — looked squarely at me, and said evenly and solidly, "We don't warm them up here."

It was a statement of fact. They didn't warm them up. You want warmed-up buns, you go to Maison Chic around the corner and smear brie on them.

The Fat Man doesn't play games. He runs a mediocre restaurant, take it or leave it, and that goes for your law firm. People who diddle around and don't order right away are left to sit a good long while because they are wasting his time. Anybody who moves a table so much as an inch from exactly where he has placed it never does it again. He gives the table a water glass–sloshing shove to get it in line, and the implication is that the next time he'll get *you* in line outside in the alley.

I have never seen the Fat Man smile. Anybody who smiles at him gets the twitchy cheek. A six-foot-plus beefy guy with a beer gut hanging over a spotted apron, forearms straining against the rolled up shirt cuffs, loses something when he smiles. He is there to serve food. That's the deal. Other waiters in the restaurant smile, but that is their problem, and his presence dominates the place. He is one with the moose heads on the wall, the dark paneling, the long, shiny bar where the regulars sit, and the narrow, tunnel-like dining room with no windows that forms the heart of the restaurant. Even when he walks from that dimly lit bar area into the adjacent square, sunny room that looks out onto the street, he carries the murky atmosphere with him. A sign on the wall of the sunny room shows a group of happy people clutching cocktail glasses and reads, "We have parties here." When the Fat Man stands in front of it, the sign looks like a warning.

But his restaurant is always crowded, and during lunch hour the lines often spill out the door and onto the sidewalk. I figure that either a lot of other people need to cling to this masochistic little island of blunt directives in a flood of double talk or, running true to Washington form, they are too absorbed in their working lunches to notice. The Fat Man has an open contempt for the working lunch. It isn't personal, exactly. It's more like a force of nature, a general scorn for the whole rather than the specific. His is not the vindictive carping of some unhappy underling who is having the screws put to him by superiors. The Fat Man is his own person, operating on his own terms. For years he has listened to the talk, watched the action, judged the city to be insane, and decided that the democratic process is no way to run a restaurant.

The Fat Man is part of a breed in Washington that I think of as "the mavericks." These are the people who live on the edge. They know Washington well, use it, kick sand in its face, and take no crap from it. *In* the city, but not *of* it, they mock its arrogance from their independent vantage points behind cash registers, in the driver's seats of cabs and subways, or merely standing on street corners.

There is a subway motorman for the city who regularly risks his job taking verbal pot shots at his riders during the evening rush hour. Being flip on Washington's Metro system is heresy and prohibited by an act of Congress. People are supposed to be quiet on the trains or speak in hushed, respectful tones so that passengers can read their *Posts* and get their work done. Metro drivers are trained to make announcements in well-modulated voices that make them sound like part of the machinery.

"Hi there, folks, and welcome to Big Red," says the maverick motorman over the loudspeaker of the Red Line train as people board at the Farragut North station. "Step all the way into the car. Come on, you can do it. Nothing bad will happen to you in the middle of the car. And remember, this entire train will reach the next station at the same time."

"Check for those briefcases and umbrellas," he says when they get off the train. "Now check again. We don't want to leave any papers on the train, do we? That's right. And thank you for riding Big Red. The time in Cleveland Park is six twenty-two. Ciao."

The voice is essentially polite and cheerful with just a hint of a sneer to it. He sits in the driver's compartment behind dark one-way glass so that nobody can see his face, but he can see all of ours. I picture him leaning back, operating the controls, thinking up his material as the car flies through the tunnels, delighting in the shocked looks of workaholics jolted out of their *Congressional Quarterlys*.

Mavericks get their jollies blowing the workaholic mind. That's why they stay in Washington. They see the tight facial muscles, the hunched shoulders, the head-down hurried walk, and think to themselves, "Go ahead — make my day."

The undisputed kings of mind blowing work for the city's nearly one hundred messenger services. Cocky, flamboyant, and untouchable, Washington messengers have taken what in other cities is a mundane job and turned it into a cult of urban daredevils. How different from the old shuffling guys who delivered packages to the *Boston Globe*'s Dorchester headquarters, offering up their packages rather apologetically, asking you to please sign if it wouldn't be too much trouble. Washington messengers are young and sleek and usually wear some neon color combination, like chartreuse and yellow shorts over black tights, which is topped off with a Darth Vader motorcycle helmet. With this ensemble and great panache they can bust into any meeting, interrupt the most confidential call, and not care who is writing what on a deadline.

Colors rippling in the wind, they race down congested streets on their ten-speed bicycles, squeak just ahead of a bus pulling out from the curb, dodge the truck, zip catty-cornered across the intersection, and weave between the construction site and the limo about to open its door. They thumb their noses at the orderly, cautious, inchworm masters they have contracted to serve by delivering the goods with an adrenaline high rarely felt in the halls of power. They mock the slow death of meaningless paper pushing with race driver skill and a lightning ride down Pennsylvania Avenue during rush hour that very few deputy assistant undersecretaries would have the guts to take.

"Hello!" they shout when entering an office, and it is more of a demand than a greeting. They know they carry the most important cargo in town — paper, without which the words would not be passed, the reports would not stack up on desks, and the stories would not be filed. They present the paper confidently and with a slight smirk, knowing that the person at the desk is panting for the document or that the person who ordered it delivered is pacing at the other end. They know that millions in taxpayer and private money is spent every year hiring them to carry paper around the streets of Washington, and they know that most of it is junk.

They heft the weighty reports titled "The Budgetary Status of the Federal Reserve System," or "Tax Policy: New Directions and Possibilities," or "World Motor Vehicle Data." They slap down the releases from the Inter-American Development Bank written in Spanish; the statements from the Royal Embassy of Saudi Arabia on what the Ministry of Petroleum and Mineral Resources had to say in Jeddah; word of a new board member at Exxon; the new urban strategy from the Conference of Mayors; the advisory from the Council on Hemispheric Affairs; and a Justice Department study on crime in Oxnard, California.

Then they call their offices for the next job and leave as quickly as they arrived, running down the carpeted halls and elevators, zipping through the lobby — bold, screaming exclamation points clashing with a subdued gray world of semicolons. Sometimes they wear silk shorts, and sometimes skintight leather. They are often seen in groups, chatting rapidly, ignoring the stares, standing tall, superior, blatantly wild. "You want your silly papers?" they say to themselves. "Okay, you'll get them — our way, in a fuchsia jump suit."

Part of the rebellion comes from a jive black culture mixing it up with a repressed white one, although mavericks come in all colors and shapes, and blacks are certainly doing the workaholic number in the corridors of power. But out on the fringe, where the young non-career-oriented find their minimum-wage niche, there is a certain style and cool that blacks in other places can't afford to have because they're not in the clear 70-percent majority. The message — not violent, not hostile, but direct from many a messenger bike and behind many a counter — is, "Babe, this is my city and my time — you want honky hustle, you go to New York." It's healthy, it's open, and it's a lot easier to take than the seething racial undercurrents of places like Boston.

Joan, who had driven a cab in Washington for six years, was a keen observer of the hustle. She told me that she had seen too many famous people and that the President of the United States could get in her cab and she'd be loose. She recalled how ABC News' Sam Donaldson got ticked off because she didn't recognize him and automatically take him to the press entrance of the White House.

"Hey," she said, half turning to me in the back seat as she maneuvered expertly through traffic, "when you've driven Liza Minnelli to the Kennedy Center, who's Sam Donaldson?" Then she told me how a group of TV honchos riding with Eric Sevareid ripped him apart as soon as he got out of the cab, and how Billy Carter griped about his brother, Jimmy, all the way to the airport.

"People tell me their troubles," said Joan, who looked to be in her mid forties, had a soothing voice, and seemed to be very easy to talk to. "They tell me their children are on drugs and their marriages are going to hell and then I drop them off at the most beautiful houses you can imagine. I say to myself, 'How can they be so unhappy living like that?' There are so many superficial, serious people. They think that's the way they're supposed to be, poor babies. I just listen, collect the money, and shake my head."

Another cabbie told me he flatly refused to pick up some of the powerful. "Say a guy flags a cab that's coming down the street," he explained. "But then the guy sees me and waves me over because he figures I can pick him up first. Well, I won't pick him up. He flagged the other cab first, and the other cab should get the fare. I don't jump just because some bigwig is in a hurry. They're not going to use me like that."

The cabbie had just had a run-in with a potential fare over this principle, and it was on his mind. He talked about it, mostly to himself and in great detail, for the entire ride from Capitol Hill downtown to Seventeenth and Pennsylvania. He was an older man and probably just this side of crazy, but he made sense. Like other crazies I've seen and heard in the city, he had worked out a logic, a policy, that when held up to the light, sounded at least as solid as much of the reasoning coming from the federal government.

Street people, grate people, protesters in Lafayette Park, and other mavericks in the extreme all seem to operate with one toe in reality. Railing, screaming, mumbling, they still have a savvy about them, almost as if they know they are reflecting a fun-house-mirror image of the other half of Washington.

"I've contacted my lawyer about this," says the man who wears the white wool cap in all weather and holds out a white Styrofoam cup to passers-by at the corner of Pennsylvania and Seventeenth. "The bombs could go off any day. My lawyer says we've got to fight them. We need help."

He walks up to people, waves the cup, and says, "You know I'm right. You know I know what I'm talking about." The voice is rapid, singsong, and the words are repeated over and over again in a kind of litany, but he is not screaming nonsense. He is saying what we all really do know. His expression is aggressive, leering, defiant, but there is that hint of sanity, and an observer gets the feeling that maybe, just maybe, this guy really does have a lawyer, or was one.

After all, how much would it take to push somebody on the three-piece-suit side of the street over the edge? A loss of access? A dive on a tax bill? Not making partner?

What about the old man in the naval captain's uniform who walks around and around the block circling the White House in slow, stately, measured steps as he mumbles about the Pentagon? Had he been there once? Is this the result of too many meetings in the Situation Room?

The Captain walks tall and in full dress with the braid on his shoulder and the medals pinned to his breast. He has a white beard, a ruddy complexion, and the faraway look of somebody who is keeping his eye on the horizon for periscopes. He looks like a ghost from World War II and would seem to be in town for a veterans' ceremony. He has a dignity about him that comes of giving commands and making decisions. Only his shoes — worn and full of holes — give him away as a street person, but he does not notice them as he makes his rounds. He isn't wandering aimlessly. He walks with a purpose, seemingly inspecting all he sees, nodding to passers-by and occasionally talking softly to himself about matters of national security.

The Photographer doesn't talk at all. He wears an army jacket and jeans and could fit right in with the press corps, except that he doesn't take any pictures. The Pentax hanging around his neck is untouched, and the camera bag he sometimes carries remains shut. He is usually sitting in a coffee shop watching people or staring out the window, smiling pleasantly. It's as if he's taken all the pictures that need to be taken and feels there isn't much point in taking more, even though every other photographer in Washington is still framing shots. He knows the truth. Enough pictures already. Let the fools keep clicking.

The Leopard Man appears to be a put-on — or is he? He has a punk hair style dyed to look like leopard spots, but that is the only odd thing about him. The rest is pure K Street. He is nicely dressed in a suit, tie, raincoat, and shiny shoes. He carries an expensive maroon leather briefcase bulging with papers. He walks quickly down the street and keeps checking his reflection in store windows. Is he an executive who has just flipped and joined the freaks, or is he a freak who has just flipped and joined the executives?

At the corner of K and Eighteenth streets the clean-cut

young man with blond hair who could pass for a Kennedy regularly holds forth, sounding as if he is being interviewed on a talk show.

"I don't play politics," he says earnestly. "I am antipolitics and I want your vote."

Down the street the sidewalk preacher at the corner of K and Seventeenth jumps and dances through the crowd of commuters, lifts his bullhorn to his lips and shouts, "Remember your soul and forget your gold! Get the sin out, get the sass out. If you're sanctified, you won't suicide." He dashes back and forth along the sidewalk, crouches down on one knee with his other leg stretched out behind him, and confronts a member of his flock. "You — I mean *you*," he says, looking up at the Burberry raincoat. "You hear me talking to you?" He jumps up again, waves his arms, taps the porkpie hat flatter against his head, and spins around to someone else. He is having the time of his life. There is an impish quality to this cheerleader for Jesus, a mischievous swagger that is almost a parody of itself or perhaps of those hundreds of legislators who do more or less the same thing on street corners in their home towns in the weeks before an election.

The jazz flute player, dressed in purple with silver streaks on his purple shoes, plays like an urban Pan on the preacher's corner, sways seductively with the music, pierces the consciousness, and demands that the emotions be recognized, however briefly, on the walk to the office. And across the street the dignified man in the suit and tie, handkerchief carefully folded into his breast pocket, stands and holds out his hat for change as he does every morning, and his bearing and the tilt of his head seem to be saying, "I am dressed as nicely as you, perhaps better. I will accept your contribution to my political action committee."

There is nothing timid about these people. They know how the town works, and they are working it. A raggedly dressed protester pushing a cause on Seventeenth Street stopped me as I hurried to the office. When I declined to accept a leaflet, the woman fixed me with a taunting look and said pointedly, "Better take it. It's not fashionable to be the last to know in Washington." She knew how the system operated. She was wise to the city's ego- and information mania. She didn't beg or talk about the great brotherhood of man needing to work together for peace. She hit me with the big guns — I'd get to the office and look stupid.

The permanent protesters bivouacked in Lafayette Park across the street from the White House have become media stars, holding press conferences and getting as much or more ink and airtime than any congressman on the Hill. Concepción Picciotto, a small and articulate woman who wears a huge gray wig and camps under a giant tent-shaped cardboard sign protesting nuclear weapons, can explain the Supreme Court decision that clamped down on White House protesters.

Her sign depicts mushroom clouds and a likeness of Ronald Reagan and the message that nuclear weapons are "a disgrace to decency, civilization, reason and logic."

A man who calls himself Thomas, and who spent years sitting in front of the White House before the Supreme Court ruling shifted him across the street to the park, had his wedding to a fellow protester there covered by the *Post*. He has dedicated his life to sitting under a sign that reads, "Live by the Bomb, Die by the Bomb." He once tried to walk across the Sinai Desert for world peace and has been arrested sixteen times for disorderly conduct and other misdemeanors. His bride, Ellen Benjamin, a former $25,000-a-year administrative assistant who chucked her career to live on the street, has been arrested seven times — once for living in a tree for ten days. These two tell the *Post*, with all the exuberance of young professionals carrying freshly minted political-science degrees, that they "naturally gravitated to Washington."

They belong here. They have a purpose. They're organized. They are part of a coalition that shouts and waves its messages amid the manicured lawns and flower beds of a national park while across the street other coalitions shout and wave their messages amid the manicured lawns of a rose garden.

This contrast is Washington's soul, its flicker of humanity in android country. On some level, however subliminal, Washington recognizes that it needs the counterculture, the alter ego, and the flip side more than most places. I think that explains the growth and attraction of the Adams-Morgan section of the city, which is a throbbing carnival of street people, festivals, block parties, and pure funk. Cross the Calvert Street Bridge from Connecticut Avenue, or head up Eighteenth Street out of Dupont Circle, and suddenly we're not in Kansas anymore, Toto. We're in the Lower East Side of New York: pushcart vendors, stores with the doors open and the owners seated on the stoop, people hanging out on corners, fortune tellers, and food of every imaginable ethnic group. The smells come from all parts of the earth, as do the languages. There is garbage in the streets and dirty words scrawled on the walls. Someone is playing a bongo drum in an alley. Out-of-control radios blare from apartment windowsills. Raucous, bold, dangerous on the dark streets, Adams-Morgan, which took its name from two elementary schools in the community — one black and one white — is a riotous affront to the cold marble and rabbit warren existence of the government that may be only a few blocks away but is in another world.

The property values are increasing here, the yuppies are moving in, as are the chic cafés, but the mavericks are not moving out. The neighborhood's motto is "Unity in Diversity," and the hard core remains to keep it honest and grungy.

This compulsion to throw off the traces that draws people to Adams-Morgan also pulls them into Georgetown on a Saturday night, but with different results. In Adams-Morgan they come to nurture a neighborhood and a psyche. In Georgetown they are part of a mob come to tear it down, or at least rattle the antiques of the gentry. Georgetown, queen of chic, where the elite have long been known to dine late in their $300,000 town houses and make decisions of state, is now called "the boardwalk of D.C." The stately homes still stand on the tree-lined side streets, the matrons have their gardens, and the Porsches and Mercedes grace the driveways, but the place is invaded by hordes thirty thousand strong on the weekends, and on weeknights, too, in warm weather. Mostly young people under twenty-five, they come to walk the streets, drink too much beer, throw up, and urinate on the neatly trimmed lawns. They patronize the fast food beer-and-taco places and move like a human tide in and out of the new-wave clothing stores, punk poster shops, and video-game arcades all built especially for them.

The swarm began hitting Georgetown around 1980. Residents attribute it to a fast-paced, permissive society; prejudices toward the area's wealth; and the drinking age of twenty-one in Virginia and Maryland that sends kids into D.C., where it's eighteen. There are also the street events — radio station WMAL's Gross National Parade, which brings seventy thousand people in weird costumes into the westernmost end of D.C. to celebrate April Fools' Day. On Halloween as many as forty thousand revelers jam Georgetown's streets, tying up traffic back down M Street and across the Key Bridge to Virginia, and bringing gridlock to Wisconsin Avenue.

William Cochran, a Georgetown architect and president of the Advisory Neighborhood Commission, recalled a summer night at a friend's house when there was so much street noise "we couldn't carry on a conversation."

"There were kids outside sitting on the cars, drinking beer, and blasting their radios," he said. "Averell Harriman lives around the corner, and I think there is something positively obscene about picturing Averell Harriman sitting in his living room unable to open a window."

Things got so bad that in 1983 Randolph Roffman, managing editor of the *Georgetowner*, wrote an editorial for the paper calling for Georgetown to secede from the District of Columbia.

"It was written tongue-in-cheek," said Roffman, "but I

really think we have to have a stronger voice in our own destiny. We can't just let the crowds walk over us."

There is a feeling one gets, wedged tightly in the throngs on a Saturday night, that they could do that — stampede and trample anybody who got in their way. There is a seething electricity, a sense of passions about to ignite which perhaps are kept bottled up all day in clerical jobs or in uniforms on military bases.

I sometimes get that feeling about the whole city and think it's quite possible that one day there will be a rebellion, a mass breaking of hermetically sealed office windows, and a cathartic flinging of computer print-outs into the street. The stunted bureaucrat will think of the Fat Man and the messengers and the flute player and that woman selling those big tomatoes in Adams-Morgan, and the night he almost bought the Johnny Rotten poster in Georgetown. The memories will explode into a frenzy of broken traces, and the newly liberated will run through the streets shouting, "Here I come, Big Red. Wait for me, wait for me!"

16

Of Pickles, Mules, and Saxophones

THE MAN WALKED into the Capitol with a plastic pickle pinned to his lapel. He smiled and handed me a button that said, "Vote for Pickles, the People's Choice."

I figured a guy named Pickles had to be running for something, or maybe two Texans, J. J. Pickle and his cousin, were running for two somethings.

"We're for pickles," the man explained brightly. "You know, as in catsup, relish, and hot dogs. We're the pickle lobby."

Of course. The pickle lobby. Where would America be without the pickle lobby? All those cucumbers with no place to go to die. All those corned beef deli sandwiches wrapped up in white paper by themselves with nothing to leak on their bread. The pickle lobby. Fascinating image. I pictured an office building where the walls around the ground floor elevators were plastered with gherkins and dills. A man dressed in green walked over and said, "Welcome to the pickle lobby. The mustard caucus is upstairs."

Spend enough time on Capitol Hill without a group to call your own and your mind will start picturing things like this, too. There is no cause too obscure, no organization too small, and no wish list too ridiculous not to have a delegation in Washington asking for it. The plywood people, the rubber people, the parking lot association people, and the folks who want Congress to pass a bill designating seven days of every calendar year National Handball Week are all here wearing lapel pins, passing around leaflets, and popping in and out of offices with the bustling exuberance of the pickle man.

This is America. This is Washington. This is America in Washington, and it can give the unorganized person indigestion, especially when one considers what could happen if the plywood, rubber, and pickle people ever joined forces and got something into a jar.

I have never been a joiner, not even during the Vietnam era. I spent the sixties in my room, confused. In 1970 when the war was winding down, I came out and sent a telegram to Richard Nixon telling him to stop the bombing. This was probably the most dramatic protest statement of my life.

Okay, okay, I went to school in Columbus, Ohio — what do you want? When I graduated from Ohio State University in 1967, guys still had crew cuts and girls were sleeping on brush rollers with those little plastic picks digging into their scalps all night. That's partly why I went into journalism — not because of the little plastic picks digging into my scalp all night, but because the profession prohibited its practitioners from joining anything. One had to be objective and stand apart. It was the perfect haven for the ambivalent.

Standing apart on the Capitol steps watching coalition after caucus after trade association going in to see its government has made me feel downright inadequate and at the same time downright disappointed and at the same time downright entertained.

You see what I mean about ambivalent?

It took me years to make a move on an issue that by all accounts is considered one of America's historical heavies. It would probably take me several lifetimes to get passionate enough about pickles to send a telegram, let alone appear in person wearing a lapel pin and smiling at strangers who might be allergic to them. And yet, here are people marching in every day, rock solid sure, dedicating their lives to import quotas and brine.

The pickle man had white hair and blue eyes. He wore a navy suit, white shirt, and dark tie. He had that long-winded enthusiasm evident in people who like committee work to go on into the night. He was here to see his representative and talk warts. I watched him walk down a corridor purposefully, confidently, and wondered if I had been missing the essential democratic experience all these years by simply going into the voting booth to pull levers instead of going down to Washington to try to pull strings. I also wondered if the democratic experience might be missing something essential, like a sense of the big picture and maybe half of its marbles.

I'm still wondering, so don't look for any answers here. All I can tell you for sure is that it is really weird seeing a bunch of government officials lined up on the east lawn of the Capitol spitting seeds for the National Watermelon Association.

They did that in July 1985 to allay any fears the public might have had after 281 people turned green from eating insecticide-tainted watermelons in California earlier that month.

"America, go out and do your thing and buy these great watermelons," said Representative Bill Cobey, Jr., from North Carolina, sounding like one of those guys who sells discount dinette sets on late-night television. "I'm going to eat one to prove it's safe."

Senator Jesse Helms, also of North Carolina, ate some, too. So did Senators Mack Mattingly of Georgia and William Roth, Jr., of Delaware; and Representatives Kika de la Garza of Texas and Bill Emerson of Missouri. And let's not forget former Secretary of Agriculture John Block, a phalanx of assorted agricultural undersecretaries, and nine state watermelon queens. They stood in a row for the seed spitting contest, and the queen from South Carolina won when she spit a seed twenty-five feet, five inches.

At times like these I always imagine a crew on a spaceship

from Mars hovering out of sight in the clouds with high-powered telescopes, getting its first impression of the United States of America.

"What are they doing?" one of the crew members asks.

"Expectorating," comes the answer.

"Are you sure this is their capital?"

"Definitely."

A month earlier the Martians would have seen eight thousand people, including members of Congress, guests, and families, standing in the courtyard of the Russell Senate Office Building eating ice cream. It was Ice Cream for America Day, sponsored by the International Association of Ice Cream Manufacturers.

"It's important to show the interns that ice cream is a pivotal part of the summer and the United States," David Cox, a legislative assistant to Senator David Boren of Oklahoma, told the *Washington Post*. Senator John Kerry of Massachusetts said, "I eat ice cream almost every day." And William Baar of the Borden Milk Company announced, "Everybody wants to be identified with ice cream."

Sure beats being identified with taxes.

It's interesting to note that while these folks were rising to new oratorical heights over dessert on the lawn, the republic was going broke in a committee room upstairs. Congress had yet to approve a budget for the next fiscal year, which would start on October 1, and members of a House-Senate conference committee had been locked away for weeks, killing each other over deficit reductions. On watermelon day they were making plans to leave town for the annual month-long August break — not to be confused with the Thanksgiving, Christmas, George Washington, Easter, Memorial Day, and Columbus Day breaks — whether a compromise was reached or not. As it turned out, a budget was passed, but everybody hated it.

And what does this tell us?

The government is a lot better at pushing watermelons than it is at writing budgets. The people in charge take forever to do anything, and when they finally do it, they give us something less than momentous. Which is as it should be, according to Norman Ornstein, a congressional scholar with the American Enterprise Institute who has been studying the beast for fifteen years.

Talking to Ornstein doesn't help ambivalence. He says everything is fine. I hate it when people say everything is fine when everything seems weird.

"Congress wasn't designed to be efficient," Ornstein told me in an interview. "It was designed to be inefficient. Efficient legislative bodies get more and more powerful, so our founding fathers designed all kinds of roadblocks to prevent that. . . . It's supposed to be a frustrating process. It's operating as it should be. Our society is set up so that if you had a minority that wanted to be heard it would be heard."

So what we've got here are a lot of ears listening to a lot of minorities. "Special interests," they are called in the biz, or "public interest groups," and their presence makes life along the Potomac nothing if not interesting.

I'm thinking of one day in particular on the Capitol steps in the spring of 1985. The prime minister of Turkey was being ushered in to address a joint session of Congress as anti-Turkish demonstrators marched with signs; as a high school band from Illinois played "God Bless America"; as students and teachers posed with their representatives; as a religious fanatic shouted that somebody, presumably his congressman, was killing God; and as a marketing team from American Cyanamid stood holding huge color photographs of cockroaches to promote a new insecticide while Representative Silvio Conte jumped up and down in an exterminator suit shouting "Squash one for the Gipper!" because the product was being manufactured in his district.

If the Martians had decided to drop down for a closer look just then, no one would have noticed. People would have simply made room for them on the steps.

You name it, it shows up here, and it's usually on the Capitol steps — either the West Front steps or the East Front steps. The building has no back, only fronts and sides. I think it was set up that way so that visitors would never feel as though they had been made to go around back with their suitcases, cameras, and causes. Everybody is out front. In the immortal words of comedian Jimmy Durante, everybody wants to get into the act, and does.

Two hundred and fifty saxophones, ladies and gentlemen — count 'em, two hundred and fifty saxophones from fourteen nations — all crowded on the West Front steps to blow Bach, Handel, and Sousa simultaneously, more or less, and flash their brass in the sun. They came on Thursday, June 27, 1985, from the meeting of the Eighth World Saxophone Congress at the University of Maryland, invited by Maryland Representative Steny Hoyer, who had also invited the Tuba Congress when they were in town. Presumably, Hoyer will eventually invite every instrument in the orchestra to play at the Capitol, and I can't wait for the kazoos.

Hoyer's peers have invited the baton twirlers, the drum and bugle corps, the marching bands, the barber shop quartets, and the church choirs. They pose for photographs with the garden clubs, the Kiwanis chapters, and the Cub Scout troops. They shake hands with the peace people, the animal rights people, the Belgian freedom fighters, and the coalition that wants to save the kangaroo.

I think this is what Congress does best — public relations. Politicians are like press agents to society. They say, "Look, I can get you in. I'll see what I can do. The country will notice you're alive." It's not as if they're selling their souls for ice cream or watermelons or saxophone music. It's more like this is all they can do, really. If you want substantive change, they can't help you, but if you want a pat on the head, a bill in the hopper, and your day in the sun, well . . . come on down! There is a tacit understanding that the big mountain-moving projects will probably never be completed, so let's concentrate on the small stuff. Let's set up National Frozen Food Day, invite the Jolly Green Giant in for some peas, and make a piece of America smile.

National Frozen Food Day was March 6, 1984. It kicked off National Frozen Food Month and it "galvanized the industry," according to the National Frozen Food Association. "It's inspirational when the Congress and President of the United States sign a bill that recognizes the work you're doing," a spokesman said.

Donald Kent, a spokesman for the American Psychological Association, said his group held seminars and news conferences around the country during National Psychology Days, from August 26 through 30, 1983. And Paul Walker, at the Northampton, Massachusetts, Chamber of Commerce, said that Calvin Coolidge Week put his town on the map. Coolidge started his political career in Northampton, and all his descendants and fans were out in force feeling good about Cal.

Whatever turns you on.

All I know about Calvin Coolidge is the photograph I once saw of him fishing in a three-piece suit and a hat. I have a feeling that "fun" was not his middle name, but that's probably fitting, since the puritan work ethic was invented in Massachusetts, quite possibly in Northampton.

In addition to making the Coolidge clan happy, the lady bountifuls on Capitol Hill have waved their magic wands to create National Meat Week, National Independent Retail Grocer Week, National Correction Officers Awareness Week, National Digestive Diseases Awareness Week, National Helsinki Human Rights Day, Family Reunion Month, National Sewing Month, National Brick Week, National Day of the Bald Eagle, National Junior Bowling Championship Week, and National Productivity Improvement Week.

That last one would be best celebrated by having Congress eliminate the practice of fiddling around with commemorative days, according to Senator Alan K. Simpson of Wyoming and Representative G. William Whitehurst of Virginia, who estimate that lawmakers spend $200,000 annually on paperwork to process this recognition legislation. Simpson and White-hurst want them to stop and cut the list down to a couple or three a year.

These guys are about as popular as the Grinch.

Several hundred commemorative requests are introduced each year, with about a third of them becoming law, and congressional aides say that giving an ear to the suggestions, whether they are passed or not, makes for good will between government and governed.

No request is too bizarre to be heard in the halls of Congress. When the contingent comes to town from Tennessee asking for Mule Appreciation Day, they listen. When the square-dance clubs arrive in full regalia — a thousand petticoats and string ties strong — promenading two by two through the congressional office buildings and asking that the square dance be made the official national folk dance, they all but rosin up the fiddle bows.

They listen to everybody, from supporters of National Margaret Mitchell Day, to Benign Essential Blepharospasm Awareness Week, to National Snowmobiling Month, to the Year of the Ocean. Your wish list is their command. In fact, New Jersey Representative Matthew J. Rinaldo is calling for National Make-a-Wish Month. The purpose would be to commemorate the Make-a-Wish Foundation, which fulfills the requests of terminally ill children.

That seems an apt analogy for the government. Washington can't cure the disease or get to the root of the problem that may be ailing the body politic, but it can make us queen or king for a day, and if we're good, maybe even send us to Disneyland.

And I don't think the so-called big-time lobbyists like Charls (no *e*) Walker or Bob Gray really fare much better with their clients' causes. Sure, the meeting may be more suave and sophisticated and involve a spread of classier food, but essentially, these grand, exalted influence peddlers are getting AT&T Day or Dupont Awareness Day or Take a

Contra to Lunch Week. Legislators simply have too many people knocking on their doors asking for too much to be able to understand any of it well, let alone push it through Congress.

What goes on in Washington is not so much influence peddling as influence gridlock. There are so many peddlers that nobody's wheels can move very fast or very far. The best that Congress can do with a crowd like this is to smile and wave or, on occasion, clap its hands together, in the style of Mickey Rooney in the old Andy Hardy flicks, and say, "Hey, kids — let's do a show!"

They did just that in the spring of 1984 when the Footwear Industries of America knocked on their door. Members of Congress and their families organized a footwear fashion show in a Washington hotel. They walked up and down a runway wearing shoes and boots that had been made in their home states, and kept smiling and waving. The finale had everybody come on stage while a professional song-and-dance lady in a sequined tuxedo outfit complete with top hat and cane sang "There's No Business Like Shoe Business."

The idea here was to draw attention to the impact foreign competition was having on the U.S. shoe industry and the need for the Federal Trade Commission to extend import quotas. As of this writing, a year and a half later, no action has been taken to aid the industry.

Undaunted, the shoe lobby and Congress whipped up the "Footprints of Power" photography exhibit in 1985, featuring pictures of the feet of twenty-seven Washington movers and shakers wearing American-made shoes. The trade association spent $40,000 on the exhibit and cocktail party and also gave participants a free pair of shoes.

Hooray for Hollywood.

Not to be outdone, the United Egg Producers came to town and put on an "Egg-stravaganza," with twenty senators and representatives from the big egg-producing states making omelets in the Longworth House Office Building.

And the International Car Wash Association, along with the National Car Wash Council, were right behind with a bash at the convention center, inviting members of Congress over for a scrub. Trying for a higher tone, this group called their party "an open forum on car detail shops." "Detail shops" apparently scrub those hard-to-reach places and provide the equivalent of a dental flossing for whatever is underneath a car.

"An open forum." I love it. Since when does Herb's Car Wash run forums? And what's with calling it the Car Wash Council? Come on. National security it's not. This is a trade group already. But apparently, many of these groups feel they've got to sound as pompous as the government to be recognized.

Consider the National Pasta Institute, for instance, the Society of American Wood Preservers, and the National Turkey Federation. These are among the three-thousand-plus trade organizations that have offices in Washington. Inevitably, there is an Association of Association Executives, and Jim Albertine of that group credits the growth of trade organizations here to the growth of government in the 1960s and 1970s.

"The government has enormous control over our lives," he said. "We need to be here to articulate our position and draw attention to our problems. We reflect what Americans do and how they do it. This is a country of people who like to organize. We like to get in groups."

Groups, groups, groups. They fill the directories of office buildings, file up to the Hill, stuff mailboxes, and mince life down to its most esoteric denominators. The Industrial Fasteners Institute, the National Pegboard Systems Association, the American Hop Dip Galvanizers Association, the Oxygenated Fuels Association, the American Society of Electroplated Plastics, the Fiber, Fabric and Apparel Coalition, the Congressional Copper Caucus, the Cling Peach Advisory Board, the International Sweetener Symposium, the Bowling and Billiard Institute of America, the National Shrimp Congress, the

Tuna Research Foundation, the Flue-Cured Tobacco Cooperative, the Washington Conference on Zinc, the Cotton Batting Institute, the Council to Save the Post Card, and the Ad Hoc Committee to Preserve Federally Assisted Short Line Railroads.

Just to name a few. And they all want to shake hands with their representatives in Congress, or at least send a note. They have gone narrow and deep into the most obscure reaches of society and formed the almighty group, and they want to be heard. Primarily, they want to be loved.

How narrow and deep do they go? Check out the following letter sent to representatives and senators in the summer of 1985:

Dear Congressman,

Transylvania lies at the very center of Romania; it is the birthplace of the Romanian nation and has been inhabited by the Romanians continuously since prehistoric times. Hungarian revisionism is morally, legally and historically unwarranted. I urge you to observe the rights of the autochtonous [sic] Transylvanian Romanians who make up practically three quarters of the population, and not try to force upon them the will of Hungarian intruders, who make up only 23.4 percent of the population. Sincerely yours . . .

What's a lawmaker to do? Get on the train for Bucharest? No, he or she simply smiles and waves to an aide to write a "thank you and we'll watch it" response, signs it with a beneficent flourish, sends it off to the heartland, and goes out to shake hands with the pickle man.

My ancestors came from Transylvania, so I should probably get excited about the Hungarian intruders and the 23.4 percent, but somehow my pulse rate is remaining fairly even. My eyeteeth aren't getting any longer, either.

What I'm thinking is that maybe I should form a group for groupless people who don't get excited about Transylvania or acid rain or Star Wars or anything much, but do suffer from a vague, indefinable malaise because they know something is really messed up somewhere, and most likely it's in Washington. We could call ourselves "The National Coalition of the Bewildered," and one fine day in the spring we could all show up on the steps of the Capitol and shrug.

It just might rattle a few congressmen, and it would certainly give the Martians a break.

17

Some Like It Hot

IT'S TIME TO BLOW the cover off one of the biggest crocks Washington has laid on the American public:

Summer.

That's right, summer. As in, "Oh, my God, it's summer in Washington and we're all gonna die." Well, we're not all gonna die. We're not even gonna breathe too hard. At least, not any harder than they're breathing in Indianapolis or Detroit or New York City or Miami or New Orleans or Lincoln, Nebraska.

So, it's summer already. Summer is hot and humid in a good chunk of America. Washington is part of that chunk. Just one more place on the map where people sweat between May and September. No big deal. No salt tablets and malaria shots. No "Dr. Livingstone, I presume?" No tsetse flies on the Mall.

A myth has worked its way into the country's consciousness, perpetuated by the country's public servants, that says the place in which these public servants work has the most brutal summers in the Western Hemisphere. The reasons for perpetuating this myth are the reasons that underlie just about everything that happens in Washington — historical precedent and ego.

In the old days people did get malaria in Washington. Of course, they got malaria just about everywhere they went. But the mosquitoes were bigger and meaner in the mud hole the federal government had chosen to call home, so when summer came people got out of town. The exodus started with European ambassadors who were not used to spending summers in mud holes with big mean mosquitoes and who fled back to their villas on the other side of the sea, screaming about the fetid air of the American swamp. Members of our government saw the ambassadors fleeing and screaming about fetid air and figured they should do the same. Europeans were considered very chic back then, and still are in a lot of quarters, and even though the country had broken away from all that chic and gentility, most people didn't want to give up the lace hankies and wigs. So, they jumped up and down, shouted "Fetid air, fetid air!" and headed for the high ground in Chevy Chase. The government was closed until fall, and a myth was born.

It never died. We have screens, air conditioning, heat-treated window glass, and computerized thermostat controls, and haven't seen a mosquito downtown since the Eisenhower administration, but every summer the "fetid air" chorus rises from the banks of the Potomac like an ancient chant and is heard abroad in the land. "We are suffering," it says. "We are giving all we've got for our country. We are tough and strong and brilliant because we are going through a trial by fire, enduring historically oppressive heat that forged the likes of Thomas Jefferson and Alexander Hamilton. You couldn't possibly be getting this stuff in Milwaukee."

There is a pride of ownership about the summer heat that people don't have about the monuments or the historical artifacts or the cherry blossom springs. The heat is personal, tangible, and macho. It pounds on people's heads, bang, bang, bang. A friend who has lived here five years says the heat is talked up as a tormentor because it makes elected officials feel oppressed — something elected officials rarely get to feel, since their job is to listen to the demands of the oppressed all day. But if they can stand on the Capitol steps in a suit and tie and long-sleeved shirt with cuff links snapped shut in high-noon July heat and sweat, preferably on camera, they feel they can get a sympathy vote or two and dispel some of the ugly rumor that has circulated over the years about their having cushy jobs.

The most I've seen people strip here was during a "balance the budget" rally on the Hill in 1982. The temperature reached the 100-degree mark, and cabinet members listening to Ronald Reagan speak went so far as to remove their jackets. But they kept their stiff white shirts buttoned up to the Adam's apple and down to the wrists, and never loosened their ties.

It stands to reason that people who spend their summers bundled up like this are going to be obsessed with talking about the heat. If they dressed in short sleeves and sandals they'd be fine. But long ago the business and political worlds established the suit as the outfit of serious intent. Men and women who wanted to go after the brass washroom key were expected to take their fashion cues from the Brothers Brooks, keeping the colors subdued, the sleeves long, and the ties tight.

In politics the outfit is for all seasons. If the budget rally had been held in January you can bet that the leader of the free world would not have appeared in an overcoat and one of those sensible hats with ear flaps. He would have stood bareheaded in a suit jacket. And the members of his cabinet would have, too. The business world has bent a little in this area and allowed for trench coats to be worn as outer garments in winter, but politicians feel that dealing intelligently with the weather is a sign of weakness. They wave cavalierly in the New Hampshire presidential primary snows. They dash from cars to receptions in the rain, smiling. The idea is to travel across America standing tall against the elements. So it figures that in the nation's capital, which is not much in the elements department, they would focus on the one season that has some weather — summer. It's not stupendous weather. It's just your average, run-of-the-mill summer, but to people who insist on going out in the noonday sun in a three-piece and who spend their time manufacturing hot air, the climate seems worthy of Dante.

I went to an embassy party one July night at which the main topic of conversation was, inevitably, the unbearable Washington summer. We were standing in a tight clump outside on a patio, drinking liquor and staring like fools at a swimming pool. The reason most of us were standing outside in a tight clump, drinking liquor, and staring like fools at a swimming pool instead of going inside to the nearly empty air-conditioned drawing room was because the "important people" attending the affair were outside in the clump. Members of Congress, key staffers, State Department officials, and of course the ambassador himself were all buttoned up, knotted in, and jacketed around out there on the patio, forming puddles.

"This is worse than my tour in Nairobi," someone said.

"You know," said a dignified-looking gentleman who seemed to think he was giving the world something for the first time, "it's not the heat, it's the humidity."

I'm telling you, just like Milwaukee. You have probably stood around your patio and had pretty much the same conversation. The only difference is that if you had an air-conditioned drawing room, you'd be smart enough to go inside and sit in it with your shoes off. Either that or you'd jump into the pool.

But people here insist on going about their usual Washington business in their usual Washington way, which tends to expend twice as much energy as is necessary and involves a lot of brisk circular footwork.

I remember sprinting back and forth between the Capitol and the Longworth Building on a string of 90-degree days when the press corps was chasing Representative Gerry Studds. The Massachusetts lawmaker had been censured for having had a homosexual affair with a congressional page, and the pack was waiting for a statement. The pack has never been known to wait calmly. We clustered outside Studds's office and ran after him whenever he went over to the Capitol to vote. Then we'd run after him when he left the Capitol to go back to his office.

On the day he held a press conference, we ran to the spot of grass out behind the Capitol where he read his statement and then ran once again back to his office. I was deep in the center of this mob but can give you no logical reason why we were running. Studds was walking and ignoring us. I think the illogical reason is that when a cameraman ran out in front to get a photo, the rest of us were spooked by the noise and stampeded after him. Also, I think we had cooked our brains spending so many days in the sun. Dripping and dizzy, with sweat smearing the ink on notebook pages, we'd catch our breaths and say, almost in unison, "Washington is hell in the summer."

Tourists standing in line for several hours, waiting to get into the White House while holding a three-year-old who needs a bathroom, say the same thing. But think about it. Anywhere you stand for several hours with a three-year-old who needs a bathroom is going to get miserable. And consider also that many of these people standing in line are from Anchorage or Seattle or San Francisco or London or other cool, damp climates where they have never heard of humidity. Suddenly, they come to the nation's capital and figure everything they've heard is true. They may even start feeling sorry for their senators and representatives.

An editor once called me from Boston asking for a story on the Washington summer. "I want sweating bureaucrats," he said. "I want you to walk around to the sidewalk cafés and watch the ice melt. I want to feel the heat bouncing off the sidewalk."

The only trouble with this assignment was that we were having a cool spell, and the temperature hadn't gotten out of the seventies for a couple of weeks.

"Oh," he said, not sounding convinced. "Well, write it next week."

This was my first summer in Washington, and every week

thereafter I kept waiting for that brutal heat so I could write about it for the folks back home. But the brutal heat never came. It still hasn't. It has merely been summer.

The truth is, Washington in the summer is mostly mental. A lot of it has to do with the inherent nearness and nature of the federal government. Just thinking about something like the federal government tends to give people heat rash. If you don't believe that, try it. Think about the IRS and the CIA and the Office of Management and Budget and the halls of Congress. Are you cool and crisp? No, you're prickly. So you can imagine what it's like living smack-dab in the middle of this stuff in the summer. The heat becomes a focal point for the frustration of a lot of people. It's the reason the form isn't processed or the promotion doesn't come through or the White House invitation isn't issued or the check is late. The heat, fueled by thousands of seething bureaucrats, fanned by the sizzling tensions of the career and social climbers, burns like a fiery pit in the mind.

And the fire is at its worst in August. That particular month in this particular city is definitely the pits. Again, not because of the weather, as legend would have you believe, but because of the aggravated mental states of the people who are unlucky enough to be hanging around town when most everybody else has left. August is evacuation month, you see — the space of time still held over from the old days when people who are considered vital to the republic are allowed to leave the mud hole in the care of those who aren't.

As you may have guessed, I have spent every August in the city. I have sat in the *Boston Globe* Washington Bureau listening to the wire machines actually slow down, and gotten worried about it. I have walked the corridors of power and seen furniture piled up in the halls, the way it is in schools when nobody is using the building. I have looked into the dead committee rooms and stared down at the silent House and Senate chambers and felt the ennui of the Capitol police watching barricades in a deserted city. I have seen parking spaces on the

Hill, and empty restaurants, and eager cabbies screech to a halt when I walk near the curb because they are so desperate for fares. I have watched reporters pack a press conference for bicyclists coming through town on a cross-country tour and ask questions about gear-shifting for a half hour because there was absolutely nothing else happening in the tri-state area. I have left the office with a hazy sun still glaring in the sky, breathed deep of the yellow, murky air, and thought evil thoughts about my fellow man.

The terrible thing about Washington in August is that it is not really a city at rest. If it was like Paris, say, where people go to the country and forget the whole deal, that would be great. But the people who leave Washington in August are always calling the office, checking up, reading lists, and giving orders to the people who didn't leave Washington. This makes for an uneasy evacuation. The body is half relaxed and half coiled at the desk, ready to spring when the phone rings. The mind is on cruise control but ready to slam on the brakes at the first sign of trouble in the underbrush. One has the feeling that one is guarding the citadel and that one could lose the whole schmear if one is not very careful. And yet, one wonders: would it matter when the citadel is so boring?

The people who don't leave Washington tend to hang out together in the deserted restaurants and talk about how deserted the restaurants are, and how bad the press conference on ten-speed bikes was, and how hot it is outside, and how much hotter it is going to be tomorrow when there will be no press conference on anything.

"It's summertime in Washington and we're all gonna die," somebody says.

"Maybe we're already dead," somebody else says.

"It's the heat," comes the answer.

"No. It's the humidity."

No, it's just Washington.

18

Homecoming

THE UNITED DC-10 was landing at Dulles International Airport, and the voice of a stewardess came over the plane's public-address system. She was giving us the usual pleasantries about weather and time, and thanking us for flying United. I was barely conscious of the voice and concentrated on holding the week's vacation in California closely around me, hoping that nothing political would wedge its way into the now wide, free western expanse of my mind.

California is my fountain of youth, an endless wellspring of the possible that cleanses the shopworn predictabilities of the probable. I need to go there every so often and breathe. I had stood on a hill in San Francisco and watched four fireworks shows at once. I had heard art lectures at Stanford University and hugged old friends. I wanted an easy landing.

The mood cracked before I reached the gate. The stewardess did it. She was ending her landing speech smoothly and professionally, much as the plane was rolling easily along the runway. "On behalf of the crew and myself, I thank you once again for choosing United and wish you a pleasant and successful evening in the Washington, D.C., area."

The word "successful" jammed in my middle ear, tore straight up into the western expanse of my mind without knocking, demanded to be recognized by the chair, and then got the whole damn vacation referred to a subcommittee on a voice vote.

In fifteen years of flying I had never heard a stewardess wish me a successful evening. Safe and happy, yes. Enjoyable, sure. Wonderful, even. But successful? Absolutely not. People landing in fun places did not want to have successful evenings. They wanted to drink piña coladas with little umbrellas in them and buy silly shirts. Obviously, I was not going to get a little umbrella and a silly shirt. I was going to get the federal government.

Did I think this was the off-season special to the Magic Kingdom or something? Had I forgotten my priorities? This was the return flight to the career ladder in the most important city in the world. The yellow pads had come out shortly after the plane had left San Francisco and had stayed on tray tables during the movie. The briefcases were out, and so were the reports. I was flying the Washington Metro in the sky. These people were on their way to working nightcaps in the Ionosphere Lounge. They would close the deal before the luggage hit the carousel.

I wanted a Dramamine. Everything was moving way too fast, and the movement seemed to be circular. The voice of the stewardess persisted. She was telling us to exit the plane and step into the "mobile lounges" that would take us to the gate.

"Mobile lounges" jammed in my middle ear and raced on up after a "successful evening." Ridiculous. Whoever heard of a "mobile lounge" anywhere else in America? They weren't lounges at all. No bar, no can, and no comfortable seats. They were vans with uncomfortable seats and no place to put luggage. So why didn't the people in charge just call them vans? Come to think of it, why didn't we taxi up to the gate in the plane the way the rest of America does at other airports? Because Dulles is Washington, that's why, and Washington is madness.

Dulles is a big, beautiful airport built in the Virginia wilderness where people do not want to go when they are in a hurry to catch planes. People want to catch planes fifteen minutes from the city at dinky, cramped National Airport. So to make the white elephant in the wilderness more inviting, state and federal planners did what they usually do when they can't think of what else to do — they built a highway. The longest bowling alley in the world now connects the Beltway with Dulles Airport, and it is called — hang on — the Dulles Access Road. Hey, to a group of state and federal planners that sounded like Mozart.

The road is exclusively for Dulles traffic, which means that anybody who gets on it by mistake must drive all the way to the airport and then turn around and come back, killing a good half hour going nowhere. But if you work for the government, you don't notice things like that. Except for a few stalwart travelers and confused motorists, the road is almost always empty. Every time I drive it, I'm convinced there has been a nuclear attack and the fallout has not yet reached the Virginia wilderness.

I hate going to Dulles, and I hate even worse coming home to it because it is not home and will never be home. I saw that more clearly than I'd ever seen it on that July evening as I took the lounge that was not really a lounge to a highway that was not really a highway into a city that was really a district. California is home. New England is home. Ohio and Florida are home. But Washington is an access road to somewhere else. It is an interim, a docking station in space where people cluster for a while and test each other. It is not a nurturing, light-in-the-window kind of place. It is a trial, a decathlon for the psyche — how far can you go, how fast can you go, how little humanity in your life can you stand?

In 1979 I had gone to California for a year on a Stanford journalism fellowship. I came back discovering I loved two coasts, East and West, with an equal passion. The easy, sensual, accepting life beyond the Sierra was as much a part of me as the puritan ethic and tight little folkways along the

Charles. But coming back to Washington from a Stanford reunion in 1985, I felt angry and slightly cheated. The nation's capital is neither East nor West. It's a chameleon, adapting to whatever is fashionable, whoever is speaking, and wherever its leaders are taking it. There is nothing solid to pound your fist against and say, "This right here, this is what bugs me," or "This is what I love." Washington is insidious, unknowable, and sly. It's the kind of place that makes Sister Boom Boom look good.

Sister Boom Boom is the gay guy in San Francisco who dresses up like a nun and goes around on roller skates preaching the gospel of "the Sisters of Perpetual Indulgence." He is West Coast insanity — direct, wild, and above all, noticed. Insanity does not couch itself in a system and pass itself off as logic out there. It is celebrated for what it is. Kooks are revered because they are kooks. The pastel houses with polka-dot trim are painted lovingly and cherished for their uniqueness. The impracticality of expensive cable cars are reveled in for the dizzying drops they take down the San Francisco hills and the views they give at the top.

Stepping into the heavy, muggy air after San Francisco's chilly but somehow more lucid fog, I felt hot and tired. It was as if I had spent a week standing on the deck of a ship looking at limitless ocean and sky and had then clambered back down into the bowels of the engine room to deal with the sweaty, grubby mechanical realities of what drives that ship.

I rode too quickly, way too quickly back along the highway that was not a highway into the city that was not a city, feeling the past week evaporate as the Washington Monument and the rest of symbolic democracy came into view. The tiny red lights at the top of the obelisk blinked silently in the night as successful evenings were being had all around me.

The next morning I awoke at 7 A.M. California time — 10 A.M. Washington time — which put me well behind my neighbors who were long gone to work and deep into successful mornings by the time I hit the shower. I picked up my *Wash-*

ington Post and *New York Times* after a week of ignoring the news and not missing it. I had stayed with a friend in San Francisco who had put the *Chronicle* and the *Wall Street Journal* next to my place at the breakfast table. She figured I needed the fix to start the morning but admitted that she hadn't read the *Journal* in months. I didn't need the fix, and ate breakfast concentrating on the foghorn sounding in the Bay and looking at her bright red geraniums.

Back in News Central the papers demanded to be read. They felt strange at my left elbow on the dining room table and the stories looked even stranger, but there was no foghorn to distract me, and the radio was tuned to a news station. This is how I had started the day for three years. News in front of me and news in the left ear. God forbid I should miss something.

The headline leading the front page of the *Post* read, "US Mulls Reprisal for Terrorism." A few inches away was "Reagan Budget Shift Irks Senate GOP." The one headline I had seen in San Francisco was above a story on the board of supervisors and read something like, "Supes Ticked Off, Take Action." How different from the people back in the engine room who were mulling and shifting, not to mention "retracting" and "intensifying."

"Packwood Retracts Threat," the *Post* announced on an inside page, and "Calls Vow to Sack Reagan Bill Over Timber Tax 'Overstatement.'" I didn't understand a word of it and didn't want to. Nor did I want to know what all the shouting was about in "Dole Intensifies GOP Friction Over Reagan's Budget Stand — 'Surrendering the Deficit' Decried."

If somebody had surrendered the deficit while I was away, maybe it was dead and I wouldn't have to worry about it anymore.

Across from the Dole story, another headline shouted, "Midgetman Missile Called Too Small." What do they expect from something called a "Midgetman"?

As the Washington press corps closed in on me again, I

tried to revive the feelings of the week before at the Stanford reunion. Reconnecting with that group, I had been pleasantly surprised that I actually liked my profession. As people stood up in seminars to ask self-critical questions and analyze what the press could do better, as they acted like normal mortals, I felt good about being one of them — something I hadn't felt for a long time. I had come to expect mostly arrogance from a room full of reporters.

During the next few days President Reagan's polyp took over the headlines, and the press went after his doctors like piranhas on a Big Mac. Of course we had to because of course it was the President, but as diagrams of his innards filled the paper, I began to long for the days of Franklin Roosevelt. Columns were written, news analyses churned out, and whole sections produced on "the President's health." It was a Washington summer, nothing much was going on, and the press corps had a crisis.

I had a headache. So, I imagine, did Reagan. Nobody can feel good picking up the newspaper and staring at his large intestine on page one.

I didn't want to read any more papers. I didn't want to work. I was definitely in a screaming funk, having what Holly Golightly in *Breakfast at Tiffany's* called "the mean reds." These should not be confused with the blues. The blues are depressing and sad and keep you on the couch all day. The mean reds get you up and out for bear on Connecticut Avenue. I walked the pavement studying faces, pinched faces moving quickly. I listened to the conversations about legal cases and business deals and lobbying. I looked at the white shirts, blue shirts, suits and jackets, buttoned down, neat, coordinated, successful, and wanted to yell obscenities in the street like the crazy people.

I was back in the swamp, and there wasn't a nun on roller skates for miles. I needed a vacation.

19

Let's Move
the Whole Thing
to Dubuque

I T   S H O U L D   B E   O B V I O U S   to just about everyone by now
that the main trouble with Washington is that it's in Washington.

Clearly, the government needs to get out of town, and I'd
like to be the first to offer to help it pack. Our founding fathers might have had our best interests at heart when they
decided to do away with the roving capital and create a one-
stop-shopping federal city, but two hundred years of living
with it should tell us something. Their first instincts were
right — better to put the government on the road and keep it
there so it doesn't get too comfortable. I say we bring back the
nomadic life for our political leaders, pile them all into a con-
voy of Greyhound buses, and send them to Dubuque.

This is not meant as any sort of slam against Iowa. Dubuque
just happens to be the most real place I can think of, and the
federal crowd is in desperate need of reality. That's why they
should travel by bus. There is something terrifically humbling
about riding in a bus, providing, of course, that it's not a campaign bus, and none of these vehicles would be. Under the
new system politicians could serve only one three-year term in
any federal job, and after that they would never be allowed to
run for anything again.

The trouble with politics today is that people in it are so obsessed with what they are planning to run for next that they can't concentrate on the job they're in. A one-shot three-year term would help focus their attention. Sure, the conventional wisdom says a person has to have a lifetime of experience to handle a national office, but the conventional wisdom should take a look around and ask itself exactly how well these lifers are doing. Maybe it's time for new blood with shorter careers and a broader perspective. People traveling across America inch by inch on a bus to a temporary capital would not be overpowered by the stultifying atmosphere of the permanent one. They would be free to think and look out the window and plan a creative year in Dubuque, which would be followed by a creative year in East Millinocket, Maine, and then possibly a creative year in Fayetteville, North Carolina.

I figure that capital cities should be selected at random in annual regional drawings, and that each region would take its turn in a clockwise sweep around the United States. If a northeastern city houses the government one year, then a mid-Atlantic city would get it the next, and a southeastern city the year after that, followed by a southwestern, a western, a northwestern, then a midwestern city, and so on. No city or town would host the federal entourage twice until all municipalities had been given a crack at being the nation's capital.

The traveling government would be small by today's standards and consist of members of Congress, cabinet secretaries, a couple of hundred civil servants, and a team of computer experts. The civil servants and high-tech crew would also be in for three-year stints and would be in charge of handling the day-to-day operation of the system, most of which would be computerized. The senators, representatives, and cabinet secretaries would work on the agenda that had been set by the voters in the previous election. Say the country had voted to have some type of immigration reform package, a balanced budget amendment, and an education bill. The players would work on nothing but until they came up with something. There would be a national vote of confidence every six months, allowing for the public to replace politicians with alternates if dissatisfied with the progress.

The problem with the present system is that progress is not a high priority. Elected officials get distracted by a million issues screaming for attention and feel they have to be making statements at three different committee hearings at once to keep their constituents happy. They run hither and thither clutching little note cards, trying to keep pace with a schedule that is essentially impossible. In addition, committees and subcommittees are continually duplicating each other's efforts, so that there may be a half-dozen energy bills being written even as there are three or four education bills and a couple of farm aid packages coming down the line. Under the new rules work would be consolidated into one group effort on the national agenda, and committees would be eliminated.

Okay, okay, that's going to upset a lot of people, most noticeably the committee chairmen, but when the big door of progress swings open, somebody is bound to get flattened behind it.

Another thing that's going to be eliminated is the federal budget. Well, not the budget per se, just congressional and presidential involvement with it. Washington spends most of the year futzing around with that sucker and is usually still futzing well into the following year. Believe me, it's got to go, preferably straight into the capable hands of computer experts trained in public finance. The way I see it, these whiz kids would work up several budget formulas, ranging from flaming liberal to middle-of-the-road to right wing, write them in plain English, and present them to America for a vote. The proposals could be viewed on personal-computer screens across the country by dialing a special 800 number, or the public could get them in the mail. Experts would be available for questions during the month before the vote, which would be taken every July. That way, the numbers would be in place long before the fiscal year ended in September, and there would be no more of those late-night muscle-flexing sessions on the Hill, with budget conferees locked behind closed doors, playing peekaboo with reporters and wasting everybody's time for months.

The idea is to create a working government as opposed to a posturing government, which is mostly what we've got now. The new feds would have to work in town halls, church basements, and trailers out back in parking lots. They would be eyeball to eyeball with the people in the country they're trying to run, standing in line with them at the post office and buying toothpaste with them at the drugstore. The public would actually see a senator pushing a cart in a grocery store. This would be good for both elected official and electorate because both might finally rid themselves of the notion that the people who run the government are somehow different from you and me or that the work is mystical, requiring the talents of the anointed with blow-dried hair. No, these are not superhumans. They are human beings who buy their socks at K Mart and pump no-lead at the filling station. And the work they do is understandable and something we should all be taking part in.

Now, if this sounds too incredibly blah and colorless for words and totally lacking in the old "Stars and Stripes Forever," keep in mind that John Philip Sousa would still be very much alive and marching back in Washington, D.C. I figure that with the business end of government working its good gray buns off in Dubuque, we could turn the nation's capital into a giant theme park dedicated to hoopla, myth, and charisma. In fact, it would probably be called Hoopla World.

The President of the United States would be here, chosen as always in a national election, but clearly accepted as a figurehead and symbol of leadership rather than a grunt who crunches numbers and grubs around with the highly technical program planning out in Iowa. We have never wanted our presidents to grub and grunt anyway. We want someone who looks good and talks good and represents America with a load of class. He or she would be the chief government spokesperson and ambassador to the world, elected on personality and style.

Presidents have been elected on personality and style for

years, but it would be nice if we finally recognized that and set the person apart for that purpose instead of expecting an economist, historian, sociologist, military strategist, and eloquent speaker all rolled into one marketable bundle with high cheekbones and a million-dollar tan. I sometimes think that our historical heroes, the Jeffersons and Washingtons and Lincolns, have fared so well over time because they weren't expected to do it all when they were in the Oval Office. Also, they never had to look good on television. They never had to look good period, except for the official portrait.

Every presidential candidate — declared, undeclared, and firm maybes — would also live at Hoopla World. A special pavilion would be built for them, where they would be able to make speeches, have debates with each other, and take a public opinion poll on the hour. The presidential primaries would be held in the pavilion, with states casting their ballots via two-way cable TV hookups. All primaries would take place on the same day everywhere in the country after a week of campaigning. This would eliminate the zoo in New Hampshire, the endless analysis of "front-runner backlash," "favored underdog status," and the rest of the baloney that anesthetizes the country for several years before anybody actually votes.

The Democratic and Republican national conventions would, naturally, be held at the Hoopla World pavilion, as would the presidential election.

Hoopla World would be a kind of Old Sturbridge Village or Williamsburg for American politics. In addition to seeing the monuments that have been here for decades, tourists could visit the Senate and the House and listen to endless windy debates as they were carried on in the old pre-Dubuque days. The debating would be done by actors, or by the people who hold elected office now. It could very well be that many of today's senators and representatives will choose to stay in Hoopla World, where they can operate much as they always have instead of biting the bullet in Dubuque. The theme park would have committees and subcommittees and, of course, stakeouts for those members of the press who chose to remain and write for the daily theme park newspaper, the *Hoop,* or for the broadcasting facility, station WHOO. Out in Dubuque the action would be covered by the local press in special dispatches to papers and networks around the country. This would give reporters who never had any hope of going to Washington the chance to cover the government and see how dull it really is.

Every day at noon in Hoopla World there would be a parade down Pennsylvania Avenue featuring the President, all known candidates for the presidency, acting members of Congress, acting cabinet secretaries, and every military band in the armed forces. Ambassadors from foreign embassies in the city would also be included, since their role has always been largely ceremonial, and the more they mix it up with figureheads the happier their home countries are. The parade would end on the White House grounds with the President making a speech in the Rose Garden and then leading tour groups through the mansion.

Of course, the park would have rides, built on the now unused land along the Potomac, or perhaps over in Glen Echo Park in Maryland. There would be a massive twenty-minute roller coaster ride called "The Boondoggle," an old-fashioned merry-go-round with painted horses and calliope called "The Campaign Promise," and a centrifugal-force contraption called "The Deficit," which leaves riders plastered against the sides when the floor drops out from under them.

Each of the office buildings housing the various government agencies and departments would be turned into a ride or pavilion. By using multimedia equipment and special effects, the Pentagon would take riders through a simulated nuclear war, while over at the Internal Revenue Service, guides would take visitors along the exact route their income tax forms travel in April, showing them where their money has gone and what it does.

The product promotions and sponsorships for special commemorative days of the week that Congress does now would continue to take place here, as would the hand shaking, photo sessions with the Cub Scouts, and constituent services. That last one would include what it has always included — running down what happened to somebody's late social security check, answering thousands of letters a week, and selling people American flags.

In case you hadn't heard, flag sales are a major industry here, with over eighty thousand a year being sold through congressional offices to people who want a piece of history. They pay anywhere from $6 to $16 to get a flag that has flapped on a pole on the roof of the Capitol for fifteen seconds, maybe twenty seconds max.

There is a flag service that does nothing but oversee the hoisting of flags on a half-dozen poles on the roof. A crew of workmen goes up there between noon and two, six and sometimes seven days a week, to raise about two hundred and fifty flags up and down and up and down. Out of the box, up the rope, down the rope, and back into the box. The boxes of flags are then loaded onto a cart and sent back down a winch to the flag room, a tiny, cramped area in the basement of the Senate side of the Capitol.

The place looks like Betsy Ross Central. Carts of flags are continually coming in — sent from members of Congress who purchase them in the House or Senate stationery stores — and carts of flags are continually going back out. There are carts going up to the roof and carts coming down. Much sorting and meticulous paperwork keeps straight who ordered what flown on which day, and which cards should say "happy birthday" instead of "happy anniversary," or "happy retirement," or "happy housewarming," or "happy bar mitzvah."

To watch the flag operation is to understand the essence of what symbolic Washington means to Americans and what Hoopla World would represent. Patriotism is a good thing; we should hang on to it. We should remember, but we should also remember that it takes a heck of a lot of time to get two hundred and fifty flags up and down flagpoles every day and that maybe laying this task on the people we expect to be brilliant about foreign policy is a bad idea.

I say we cheer and cry and hoist flags and feel proud in Washington, but we make the system work in Dubuque. Is that so crazy?

Look at it this way — is it any crazier than what we've got now?

20

The Outsider's Insider

WHY DID I MOVE to Washington if it's so terrible, and why do I stay?

Because it is there.

Why have Americans always come to Washington? To see it, feel it, touch the inscriptions on the walls, pretend they are Jimmy Stewart, and find out who they really are.

Washington is an irresistible force, like Moby Dick. We love it and we hate it and we come to see how good it is and how bad it is. New York is that kind of city. So are Los Angeles, Las Vegas, and Dallas. These places are bigger than themselves. They are symbols that stand out on the physical and psychic map of the country like blazing billboards, taunting, humbling, enraging, and testing us. Washington is probably more like that than the rest of them because it also lays a guilt trip on us. After all, we never voted to send anybody to Las Vegas. But every time we raise our fists in frustration at "what they did in Washington" we realize they did not do it alone. We stand facing mecca with mixed emotions, proud of our past, angry at our present, and ashamed of ourselves for not having a firm fix on what our representative looks like.

Announce that you are moving to Washington and a crowd

gathers. Friends, colleagues, enemies, and total strangers want to get involved. It's as though they are making up for lost time and past guilts over not understanding the federal government by focusing very hard on something they can understand — a human being packing a car. You become "their person in Washington." They watch with hope, fear, cynicism, and envy. They slap you on the back, nudge you in the ribs, and say, "This will be a tremendous experience," or "You have got to be stark raving out of your gourd." They shake their heads and offer lectures on the corruptibility of power, and then dig in their pockets for some home numbers of the powerful. Seeing a person they know move to Washington is much more than witnessing a simple job transfer. They are watching the beginning of an odyssey, a journey to the center of the earth, a trip back to ninth-grade civics class, a pilgrimage to the very roots of democracy.

Leaving Boston for Washington — with the car packed and the purse full of phone numbers and the mind full of enthusiasm and doubts — I felt as though I'd just been elected to something, although it wasn't clear what. I was about to go and live with the eccentric uncle I'd heard about all my life but had never met, and report back on what he was like. He couldn't be that bad, I figured, and I was right — he wasn't.

He was worse.

Uncle Sam turned out to be a maddening, calculating, arrogant, paranoid, officious, self-absorbed little snob. He also showed himself to be idealistic, enduring, noble, free, and hilarious. Either way he is family — the best of us and the worst of us and one with us. He takes a lot of getting used to, and working at it full time since 1982, I have gotten used to him and still am getting used to him. We will never be bosom pals, but we do coexist fairly well — he, preoccupied with taking care of business, and me, studying the family album for the threads that connect us while simultaneously wanting to rap him a couple of good ones in the mouth every few hours.

I have settled into a niche as everyone must in Washington

219

to survive. I have found that sliver of comfortable ground and an expertise that allows me to feel knowledgeable about something important. After several years of groping for an identity, I have learned to appreciate the beauty of the grope as an identity in itself. I have become an outsider's insider, which means I have the inside track on being out of it. And if you're an outsider planning to move to Washington, or one who is already here and feeling like an idiot, it means I can help you be a better one.

Reading this book, you may have gotten the impression that Washington is no place to live. On the contrary, the town can be quite exhilarating if you are in the right frame of mind and wearing a good set of shin guards. You just need to find your group. There aren't many outsider insiders here — six at last count — but we do exist and want to hear from you before the insiders get to you. The goal of all outsider insiders is to swell the ranks of the uninitiated, so that eventually the majority of people living in Washington won't be afraid to say they have no idea what's going on and that it's not their fault — even if they are at a State Department briefing sitting right next to Bernard Kalb.

At the rate outsiders are coming to live in Washington, we should be able to make our move sometime in the next millennium, probably during an ice age. Word has it that the polar ice cap is moving, so it's only a matter of time, and we want to be ready.

The first step you need to take if you are interested in this movement is to determine which side of it you're on. That may sound simplistic, but in Washington nothing is simplistic. The insider/outsider thicket can get particularly thorny because who or what is "in" constantly changes, depending on the news, fashion, rumor, or whim. You may be "out" today, but only temporarily, and conversely, "in" only temporarily. The important thing is how you feel about it. Anybody who wants to play the game, whether "in" at the moment or "out," is essentially an insider personality. Anybody who doesn't know there's a game going on and can't find the scoreboard is essentially an outsider personality and had better learn to like it out there.

If you're an insider, you'll act like one. For starters, you won't be reading this book. You'll be deep into Henry Kissinger. You will be convinced that your move to Washington is doing the most good for your career. You will have owned a leather briefcase since freshman year in college, and you will understand politics.

You people should stay home.

Politics is one of the more misguided activities ever undertaken by the human race, but somehow it caught on. So did smallpox, but we managed to get rid of that. I figure we're just not trying hard enough with politics. Too many of us are infected, and we keep passing it around. It's all that hand shaking, back slapping, and baby kissing. It's all those insiders running in tight little packs and sharing the same microphones.

Insiders have been that way since kindergarten and should stop now and take a break. They have always sat in the front row with their hands up in the air, bucking for president of student council, landing the big job, jogging five miles every morning, and generally ruining an otherwise nice country for the rest of us.

Outsiders sit around and eat Cheese Curls. They aren't sure they're outsiders, but they know something is wrong and are trying to decide if they care. If you don't own a leather briefcase, have had vague feelings of inadequacy all your life, and can't remember who is chief justice of the U.S. Supreme Court, you are going to have a tough time of it in the federal city, especially if you're a lawyer. You are probably coming here out of a sense of curiosity more than anything else and some sort of notion that everybody should try to understand the government.

Poor babies. You're going to need all the help you can get. The following hints for Washington living are designed to give you some of the tools for basic survival. They won't answer all your questions, or even half of them, but they will help create the proper mental attitude for accepting ignorance. And they should help mark time until the millennium passes.

1. *Picture them in their underwear.*

My mother always used to tell me this whenever I had to do anything scary in school, and it works, sort of. You look at whoever you have to look at and picture the person or persons standing there in something white, baggy, and wrinkled that came from a sale table at Sears. We're not talking Bloomingdale's monogrammed here. You get the wrong image going and you'll be in worse shape than you were before you started. You've got to think loose elastic, gray around the waistband, tank top undershirts, and Playtex Long Lines.

I once pictured the entire House of Representatives in its underwear. Tip O'Neill, Jack Kemp, Mo Udall, Dan Rostenkowski, Jim Wright, Pat Schroeder, and Geraldine Ferraro — they were all there conducting the nation's business in fashions by Sears. It was my first day on the Hill, and I found the images comforting. They were even more comforting in the Senate.

2. *Never go to the top.*

This will be relatively easy for an outsider and is an excellent way to outmaneuver the insiders who are busily trying to ingratiate themselves with power. The bottom actually knows a lot more than the top. At least the people down there can explain what they know in English. People upstairs suffer from vertigo and can't speak coherently. Just about every time I've had to interview the senator or the representative or the agency secretary, I have come away with unintelligible notes and a tension headache. These people only know the grand speech. They don't do specifics. If you want specifics and want to go to sleep at night feeling that you have made contact with fellow human beings during the day, cultivate the obscure types who never get quoted in the *New York Times*.

3. Do the balcony yell.

After a particularly harrowing day, find a friendly balcony on a high-rise apartment building — no, you're not going to jump — walk out there, and yell the following at the top of your lungs: "This city sucks duck eggs!" If you have some other appropriate phrase you prefer yelling, feel free to improvise, but be sure to walk back inside the apartment quickly and shut the drapes before the neighbors call the cops, which could serve to make your day even more harrowing.

The balcony yell offers a great release of tensions. Even if you have been dutifully picturing people in their underwear all day, you still will not have been able to vent properly because these people don't know that you're picturing them in their underwear. Tell them, and you will ruin the entire exercise. Every time they see you after that they will say, "Picturing me in my underwear again? Heh-heh-heh," and have the upper hand. But sometime during the day you will need to tell them in colorful, spirited language how frustrating it is for an outsider trying to cope with a city of insiders. On the balcony late at night is the perfect place.

4. Start a cockroach caucus.

If you live in a Washington, D.C., apartment or town house, you are going to have cockroaches. Face it/them. This is a fact of federal life, much as people don't like to admit it. They think their move to Washington will be all pink and white cherry blossoms and gleaming marble. They think the Pentagon can take care of anything that moves. Wrong. The city is bugged in more ways than one, and you can establish yourself as an independent thinker at any gathering by dealing openly with what is on everyone's mind because it is in everyone's kitchen. Just launch right into the subject and tell them what you saw running along a baseboard that morning. Put an arm around their shoulders and say simply, "Look, I've had cockroaches since I moved here, and I know you've got them, too, so let's talk." Save yourself from the terrible pressure of thinking you are the only person in town with "the problem" and that it reflects on your upbringing. Remember that ambassadors and cabinet secretaries and the President of the United States all have cockroaches. Remember that they are as indigenous to the capital as politicians, and just as persistent. Remember that you can control them, but you will never get rid of them.

5. *Talk to tourists.*

This is generally a terrific ego boost because these people know nothing. Tell them where the Washington Monument is, and they'll think you should run for president. It should be noted that it's a good idea to review the guide books for the best route to the Washington Monument before talking to tourists, or you'll wish you hadn't gotten involved. I once decided to help a group out that was looking for K Street. I was directing them the wrong way when a couple of insiders came along, took us all for a tour group from Yonkers, and told us we were standing on K Street.

If you're unsure of yourself, just hang around museums and monuments and listen to tourists talk. They discuss normal things, like lunch and film and T-shirts, and will make you feel real. They tend to stand in awe of history. They flood the Lincoln Memorial at night, aim a camera with a flash cube at the Capitol two miles away, shoot, and think they've got something. They walk in silent lines past the blackness of the Vietnam Memorial, giving it life. They head back to the row of hulking tour buses that growl impatiently along the curb and take their seats, eager for the next stop. Tourists will put you in touch with your roots.

6. *The zoo and you.*

Many a Washington outsider has found solace at the National Zoo. Just being in a place that is actually called the National Zoo is refreshing and kind of puts things in their proper perspective. The animals, particularly those in the monkey house, take on familiar personalities, and have a wise, "we've seen it all" look. It is good for the soul to walk the wooded paths, sit at grubby picnic tables drinking sticky liquids from paper cups, and eating hot dogs from foil wrappers.

I remember, one Sunday in July, sitting at a table and looking up in the trees, watching a colony of pigeons on the branches. The birds had scattered themselves, so that every table was in a direct line of fire should a pigeon decide to be indiscreet. People sat with their hot dogs and kept looking warily upward but did not move. I had the feeling that we were all thinking, "This is Washington for you, but at least we'll know where it's coming from."

The zoo has snakes and wolves and weasels and magpies and rare birds and odd ducks and strange bedfellows. It has an oryx, standing alone on his little slope of grass, not caring if he's weird or if the giraffes can see a lot more.

And it has a clock that doesn't work. I have spent a lot of time looking at the clock. It is an elaborate structure near the Connecticut Avenue entrance to the park. There are carved animals on it that are supposed to turn around when the carillon plays and the chimes strike the hour. What happens — at least, what's happened whenever I have stood waiting for the clock to dance — is nothing. Absolutely nothing. A crowd forms, looks up expectantly, and gets frustrated. There is a bench in front of the carillon and a door that leads into the glass-enclosed area surrounding the bench, but still nobody is sure whether the works will go electronically, or whether some carillon expert will appear to make it run, or whether one of us should scale the sides, fling open the door, and get the thing moving.

We stand and watch for a while, and then give up and go look at the pandas. After all, they're a much better show, and they're recognizable television personalities. As Simon and Garfunkel once said, "It's all happening at the zoo."

7. *Stop trying to figure out how a bill becomes a law.*

This one hung me up for several years until I realized no one really knows how a bill becomes a law, least of all the people passing the legislation. It just happens sometimes, that's all. Like hailstones.

That is the essence of Washington life. Despite all the planning and regulations and procedures and protocol, it just happens. There is no Truth, no answer, and no way to get to the bottom of things because there is no bottom, only points of view. When I first came here, I naively envisioned a six-month-to-one-year break-in period, after which I would understand how the pieces fit together. It would be like learning about companies in Massachusetts when I worked for the *Globe*'s Business pages. Everything is understandable if you ask enough questions. There is always a bottom line. But the federal government does not run so neatly. The pieces aren't supposed to fit together at the molten core of a democracy. They're supposed to cook and steam and fly around and make noise.

If I had to pick a symbol for the town, it would have to be one of those small crockery containers sold in a gift shop on Pennsylvania Avenue. Written on the front of the container, which could serve as a sugar or candy bowl, are the words "Current Realities." That's Washington. They'd have trouble selling "Current Realities" in a shopping mall in Kansas, but along the boulevard of broken promises, the crockery goes like the proverbial hot cake. Here the message makes sense. Here people ask what time it is, what the weather is going to be, and what the current reading is on reality.

One day the reality is war between Congress and the White House. The next day it's reconciliation for the good of America. In the morning it's the paralyzingly dry and tedious budget process, and in the afternoon it's busloads of Vietnam veterans or Holocaust survivors or crusaders for peace flooding the streets with almost unbearable emotion. The tour groups walk the halls of the Capitol and listen to guides in red coats talk of great moments in the history of the republic as a lone representative stands on the House floor mumbling gibberish to an empty chamber. A person has to learn to love schizophrenia to live in Washington because the nation's capital can give you patriotic chills as easily as it gives you the cold shoulder, and sometimes it does both at once.

So don't look for the Answer. Just look for today's answer, or the hourly answer, or best of all, your own answer. Know that living here for a while is worth the frustration and the price of admission because most of the citizenry never gets this close to their government. "Are the people in Washington nuts?" they wonder. You don't have to ask that question. You've seen them.

And years from now, on a quieter day in a saner place, standing at the picket fence listening to the neighbors puzzle over this or that craziness that has drifted outward across the land from the banks of the Potomac, you will be able to smile knowingly and tell them about the most important city in the world.

"Ah, yes, Washington," you will say, looking sagely off into the distance. "I was at the briefing."

DATE DUE